Transforming Pastors

Transforming Pastors

Spiritual Guidance through the Labyrinth of Leadership

Stephen W. Robbins

RESOURCE *Publications* • Eugene, Oregon

TRANSFORMING PASTORS

Copyright © 2016 Stephen W. Robbins. All rights reserved. Except for brief quotations in critical publications or reviews, no part of this book may be reproduced in any manner without prior written permission from the publisher. Write: Permissions. Wipf and Stock Publishers, 199 W. 8th Ave., Suite 3, Eugene, OR 97401.

Resource Publications
An Imprint of Wipf and Stock Publishers
199 W. 8th Ave., Suite 3
Eugene, OR 97401

www.wipfandstock.com

Paperback ISBN: 978-1-5326-0655-7
Hardcover ISBN: 978-1-5326-0656-4

Manufactured in the U.S.A.

Unless otherwise identified, all Scripture quotations in this publication are taken from the New American Standard Bible (NASB), © The Lockman Foundation 1960, 1962, 1963, 1968, 1971, 1972, 1973, 1975, 1977.

To
All past, present, and future pastors and Christian leaders
served by RobbinsNest Ministries

For
"Your progress and joy in the faith"
(Philippians 1:25)

TABLE OF CONTENTS

Introduction i

   1. Christ Formed 2
   2. Comedic Sense 4
   3. Holy Habits 6
   4. Restful Trust 8
   5. Integrated Self 10
   6. Spirit's Leading 12
   7. Table Fellowship 14
   8. Be 16

   9. Scaffold for Building Leaders 20
10. Service to Others 22
11. Confront with Care 24
12. Abide in Christ 26
13. Fruit-bearing Friend of Jesus 28
14. Outcast in World 30
15. Listen with Care 32
16. Devotion to God 34

17. Core Values 38
18. Christ-Centered 40
19. Orthodoxy/Orthopraxy 42
20. Mobile/*Missio Regni Dei* 44
21. Path: Vision. Intention. Means. 46
22. Affordable/Accessible 48
23. Small Churches 50
24. *Soli Deo Gloria* 52

25. Magnify Your Office 56
26. Physician of the Soul 58
27. Administrator of the Keys 60
28. Shepherd of the Ekklesia 62
29. Teacher of the Truth 64
30. Overseer of the Church 66
31. Role Model of Holiness 68

32. Eschamation Points 72
33. Preparation 74
34. Repentance 76
35. Encouragement 78
36. Adoration 80
37. Community 82
38. Humility 84

39. Kingdom Pastors 88
40. The Call 90
41. What Do You Expect? 92
42. Simply Fi 94
43. Followship in the Fellowship...96
44. What's in Your Message?...98
45. Reliable Pattern 100
46. H.o.n.e.s.t. Evaluation 102
47. Care to Focus and Focus to Care 104

48. Adventuality..108
49. Spiritual Formation 110
50. Writing a "Rule" for Life 112
51. So What's Leadership 114
52. Pastorinth 116

Appendix
Watch for Transforming Habits 120
Scaffold for Building Leaders (John 13–17) 121
Write Your Own Eulogy 128
"I Magnify My Office" (Litany of Affirmation)..130
Olivet Discourse (Matthew 24–25)...132
The Fifty-Two "Although . . . RobbinsNest Thinks . . . Because . . ." Thesis Statements 137

Works Cited 143
RobbinsNest Ministries..145
Books by Stephen W. Robbins 147

INTRODUCTION

Transforming Pastors presents fifty-two Bible-immersed, field-tested, discussion-welcoming, one-page handouts that offer *spiritual guidance through the labyrinth of leadership*. This manual draws attention to abiding and weighty themes for both emerging and seasoned leaders.

Transforming Pastors escorts you through the twists and turns of leadership to the center of ministry and returns you to a world that God so loves. There are no shortcuts. Stay on the ordained path with discipline and patience and you will experience amazing grace every step of the Way.

Each topic in this leadership manual can be considered individually or, better yet, discussed in a small group setting (e.g., with a clergy small group, church staff, elder board, missions team, etc.). Either way, be prepared to reflect upon and respond to the path of *Transforming Pastors*.

Each one-page handout covers one topic. And each topic comes with a three-line thesis statement that follows an "Although . . . RobbinsNest thinks . . . because . . ." formula. For example: Although jokes about pastors are in vogue and many in and out of the church belittle their position, RobbinsNest thinks it is high time to magnify the office of pastor and to dignify their sacred call because they are shepherds of the very ones that God purchased with His own blood (Acts 20:28)!

RobbinsNest plans to post additional material related to *Transforming Pastors* on its website (www.RobbinsNestMinistries.org)—for example, links to videos and podcasts connected to each topic (an "E-Manual"). Even a deck of cards featuring all fifty-two theses will be made available.

A big "thank you" goes to the pastors and Christian leaders across several denominations that month after month, year after year, made use of these pattern-ladened, acrostic-crafted handouts in their RobbinsNest Institute clergy cohort groups and "B.E. [Blue Egg] Pastors" small groups.

Those who have spent time with Dallas Willard in person or in books will hear his voice echo throughout this manual. He blessed me by speaking at my ordination, serving on RobbinsNest's Advisory Board, endorsing my first book, and serving on my wife's Ph.D. discertation committee.

Additional thanks goes to Oscar Orozco and John Smyser. Their custom artwork enriches the manual's looks and lessons. Public and stock paintings and photos were acquired from the Internet. Finally, all glory goes to God whose Word lights our path throughout the labyrinth of leadership.

Soli Deo Gloria!

Pastor Steve

Stephen W. Robbins

The following eight handouts focus on what it looks like to have Christ formed in you. The double acrostic of "C.h.r.i.s.t. F.o.r.m.e.d." will help guide you through this section of the labyrinth of leadership.

Do write on the handouts as you encounter questions to ponder and spiritual exercises to engage in. And use the "Reflecting on the Labyrinth of Leadership" pages to take notes, write down your thoughts, and, yes, doodle.

*Take note that the "Watch" graphic on the "Holy Habits" handout is included in the Appendix (enlarged).

CHRIST FORMED

". . . until Christ be formed in you" (Galatians 4:19).

Although "trend-winds" of change sway the targets of success and confuse both clergy and laity, RobbinsNest thinks a pastor's labor focuses to see Christ formed in themselves *and* their people because this is the essence of and pathway to "progress and joy in the faith" (Philippians 1:25).

What does it mean to be Christ-formed? How do we image forth God-in-the-flesh with all our parts (i.e., our thoughts, feelings, choices, actions, relationships, etc.) as we journey throughout the labyrinth of life and ministry? What does *"Christ be formed in you"* mean? It means that . . .

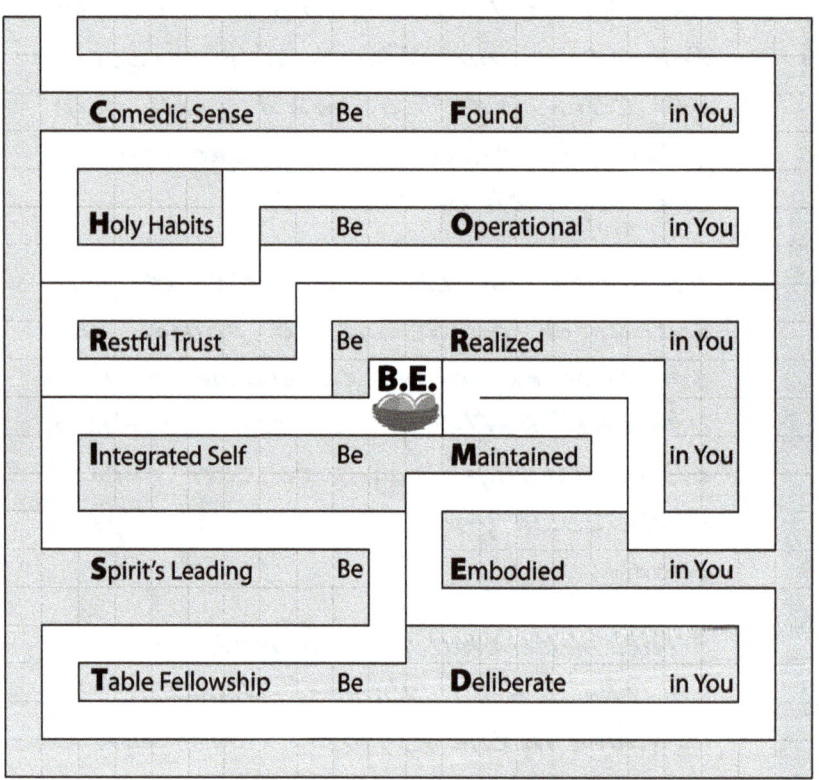

What does it mean to be Christ-formed *socially*? (2 Answers: Comedic Sense & Table Fellowship)
physically? (2 Answers: Holy Habits & Spirit's Leading)
spiritually? (2 Answers: Restful Trust & Integrated Self)

Socially ⊃	Share Joy*	Love Your Neighbor as Yourself	Confront the World
Physically ⊃	Seek Righteousness*	Love God with Mind & Strength	Confront the Flesh
Spiritually ⊃	Know Peace*	Love God with Heart & Soul	Confront the Devil

* *"The kingdom of God is . . . righteousness and peace and joy in the Holy Spirit"* (Romans 14:17).

Question: Whom do you know is advanced in being Christ-formed? What do you see in him/her?

Reflecting on the Labyrinth of Leadership

RobbinsNest Ministries
Stop. Look. Listen.

COMEDIC SENSE

"There is an appointed time . . . to laugh" (Ecclesiastes 3:1, 4).

Although we are not prone to dwell on or even consider the idea of Jesus having a comedic sense, RobbinsNest thinks it is important to recapture the true humanity and winsomeness of our Lord because love for neighbor will not fully happen until all characteristics of Christ be formed in us.

While we journey through the labyrinth of life, let's expand our **V**ision of Christ's comedic sense. Here are 5 reasons why we can expect to find a comedic sense, that is, a sense of humor in Jesus:

Heresy that is called Docetism	Jesus was fully human; not one merely seeming to be a man.
Useless argument from silence	The Bible never says He laughed, but nor does it say He bathed.
Marriage supper of the Lamb	Can you imagine a banquet without laughter? (cf. Rev. 21:6-9)
Overstatements when teaching	"First take the log out of . . ." & "Easier for a camel to go . . ."
Reputation as one eating, etc.	Sinners enjoyed His company (Matthew 11:19) & so did kids.

While we journey through the labyrinth of life, let's build our **I**ntention to have a comedic sense. Here are 2 reasons why it is important and a blessing to have a comedic sense be formed in us:

Shows forth child-like humility
Images forth God's happiness

While we journey through the labyrinth of life, let's engage in **M**eans of transforming habits:

Play and banter for re-creation
Laughter and smiles and wit
Awareness of our incongruities
Yearn to demystify knowledge

TRUE OR FALSE

- ○ True ○ False   God is happy.
- ○ True ○ False   Creation is God at play.
- ○ True ○ False   God loves a sidesplitting giver.
- ○ True ○ False   Jesus raises a smile, not bile, with humor.
- ○ True ○ False   Humor existed before the fall.
- ○ True ○ False   God gets the last laugh.
- ○ True ○ False   You are happy.

B.E. [Blue Egg] Pastors Ponder:

- How can we redeem our humor and play and entertainment?
- Why was Jesus' 1st miracle changing water into good wine?
- What would we gain by Jesus *not* having a comedic sense?
- "Strain out a gnat and swallow a camel" (Matt. 23:24): Really?
- God prescribes a joyful heart as good medicine (Prov. 17:22).
- Comedic sense & table fellowship help us love our neighbor.
- Imagine yourself there in the scene portrayed in the painting.

Reflecting on the Labyrinth of Leadership

RobbinsNest Ministries
Stop. Look. Listen.

HOLY HABITS

"Discipline yourself for the purpose of godliness" (1 Timothy 4:7).

Although the gospel gets reduced to "pray this prayer so that when you die you go to heaven," RobbinsNest thinks being born from above anticipates having holy habits be operational in us because salvation involves giving God our life (not just our death) and seeing Christ formed in us.

While we journey through the labyrinth of life, let's expand our **V**ision of Christ's holy habits. How was it possible for Jesus to be tempted in all things as we are and yet not sin (Hebrews 4:15)?

Answer: He was PREPARED. Can you see that His spirit was willing *and* His flesh was strong?

****
TRUTH @ GRACE

Grace is opposed to earning, but not to effort. Most certainly, without Christ we can do nothing (John 15:5); but if we do nothing, it will be without Christ; because grace is God acting in our lives to bring about what we do not deserve and cannot accomplish on our own.

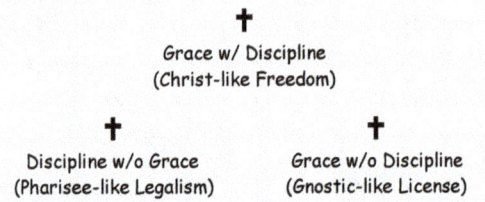

Grace w/ Discipline (Christ-like Freedom)

Discipline w/o Grace (Pharisee-like Legalism)   Grace w/o Discipline (Gnostic-like License)

Like at Calvary, there are two thieves. For humanity, like a drunkard, falls off a horse on one side, then on the other.

****

While we journey through the labyrinth of life, let's build our **I**ntention to develop holy habits. Why engage our bodies in spiritual disciplines and seek to have holy habits operational in us?

Answer: So we can be BATTLE-READY. Can you see your spirit willing *and* your flesh strong?

****

While we journey through the labyrinth of life, let's engage in the various **M**eans of grace available to us.

****

TRUE OR FALSE

1. ___ You can be Christ-formed w/o transforming habits.
2. ___ Spiritual disciplines are wisdom, not righteousness.
3. ___ The goal is to do as many disciplines as possible.
4. ___ All spiritual disciplines involve our physical bodies.
5. ___ You stumble by chance into being Christ-formed.
6. ___ You cannot be Christ-formed by direct effort.

Reflecting on the Labyrinth of Leadership

RobbinsNest Ministries
Stop. Look. Listen.

RESTFUL TRUST

"For what does it profit a man to gain the whole world, and forfeit his soul?" (Mark 8:36)

Although the burden to succeed and the need to please "seekers" presides over today's pastors, RobbinsNest thinks pastors can abandon outcomes to God and have restful trust realized in them because, like Him whom they're yoked to, they have a Father who works for, in, and through them.

While we journey through the labyrinth of life, let's expand our **V**ision of Christ's restful trust. He came to serve people, but not on their terms. He came on a mission, but entrusted results to God.

When did Jesus say "No"?
(Explicitly or Implicitly)

1. When the Gerasene demoniac wanted to accompany Him
2. _____
3. _____
4. _____
5. _____
6. _____
7. _____
8. _____
9. _____
10. _____

While we journey through the labyrinth of life, let's build our **I**ntention to realize restful trust. Imagine living with no hurry (in Jesus' time zone ☺) with a peace that surpasses comprehension!

Lectio Divina
(Read slowly and ponder the link between restful trust and the peace of God.)

"(4) Rejoice in the Lord always; again I will say, rejoice! (5) Let your gentle spirit be known to all men. The Lord is near. (6) Be anxious for nothing, but in everything by prayer and supplication with thanksgiving let your requests be made known to God. (7) And the **PEACE OF GOD**, which surpasses all comprehension, will guard your hearts and your minds in Christ Jesus." (Philippians 4:4-7)

While we journey through the labyrinth of life, let's engage in the **M**eans of grace available to us. When we take on the "easy yoke," one transforming habit we learn to practice is "Sabbath Rest."

Sabbath Day is Father's Day. We enter His rest (Hebrews 4:9-11), His peace, with restful trust and realize that we don't have to shoulder the burden; we can lay down the burden to make *it* happen.

[Jesus speaking] *(28) "Come to Me, all who are weary and heavy-laden, and I will give you rest. (29) Take My yoke upon you, and learn from Me, for I am gentle and humble in heart; and you will find rest for your souls. (30) For My yoke is easy, and My load is light." (Matthew 11:28-30)*

Reflecting on the Labyrinth of Leadership

INTEGRATED SELF

"You shall love the Lord your God with all your heart, and with all your soul, and with all your mind, and with all your strength. . . . You shall love your neighbor as yourself" (Mark 12:30, 31).

Although self-help gurus encourage us to experiment with new identities when finding ourselves, RobbinsNest thinks an integrated self, one that's whole and authentic, must be maintained in us because being Christ-formed encompasses all of our parts, every dimension of our human lives.

While we journey through the labyrinth of life, let's expand our **V**ision of Christ's integrated self. All of the essential parts of Jesus' human self were organized around and at home in His Father.

Words of Wisdom

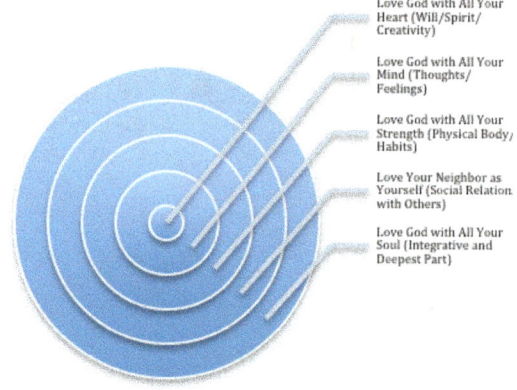

"If you are going to be transformed, you have to transform your parts. One of the things that defeats Christian growth is failure to attend to the parts of the person. . . . Take care of the parts, and the whole will take care of itself. Missing this will lead to a life of frustration. It will lead to a life of failure, because you'll keep trying to change you without changing your parts, and you can't do it." (Dallas Willard, *Living in Christ's Presence*, 116-7)

While we journey through the labyrinth of life, let's build our **I**ntention to maintain an integrated self. With integrity and a 24-7-365 commitment, we unite and live in God's kingdom among us.

"For Your Glory, Lord, I/We Live"

The devil wants "to split" you!

- Your relationship with your God
- Your relationship with your spouse
- Your relationship with your kids
- Your relationship with God's Church
- Your relationship with yourself!

How does the enemy try to split you?

_____
_____

While we journey through the labyrinth of life, let's engage in the **M**eans of grace available to us.

Heart	"Where your treasure is, there will your heart be" (Luke 12:34).	**I** [i]nitiate/create
Soul	"Take My yoke . . . & you shall find rest . . ." (Matthew 11:29).	**X** [ch]ill out/rest
Mind	"Be transformed by the renewing of your mind" (Romans 12:2).	**Θ** [th]ink / notice
Strength	"Present your bodies a living and holy sacrifice" (Romans 12:1).	**Y** [h]abits ← good
Neighbor	"Be subject to . . . [&] serve one another" (Eph. 5:21; Gal. 5:13).	**Σ** [s]ubmit/serve

Reflecting on the Labyrinth of Leadership

SPIRIT'S LEADING

"Then Jesus was led up by the Spirit into the wilderness to be tempted by the devil" (Matthew 4:1).

Although the third member of the Trinity is often misunderstood, downplayed, or even ignored, RobbinsNest thinks the Holy Spirit's leading is to be embodied (welcomed and manifested) in us because kingdom living is "righteousness, peace, and joy in the Holy Spirit" (Romans 14:17).

While we journey through the labyrinth of life, let's expand our **V**ision of the Spirit's leading embodied in Christ. Jesus knew the Spirit to be a living Person ("He") to come alongside Him for comfort and guidance, not a doctrinal system ("it") to define and manipulate for His agenda.

> Jesus was conceived by the Holy Spirit (Matthew 1:18; Luke 1:35), baptized by the Holy Spirit (John 1:32-33), led by the Holy Spirit (Luke 4:1), anointed by the Holy Spirit (Luke 4:18; Acts 10:38), and empowered by the Holy Spirit (Matthew 12:28). Jesus offered Himself without blemish to God as an atonement for sin by the Holy Spirit (Hebrews 9:14), was raised from the dead by the Holy Spirit (Romans 8:11), and gave orders to the apostles whom He had chosen by the Holy Spirit (Acts 1:2). (See *Transforming Beliefs*, page 77)

While we journey through the labyrinth of life, let's build our **I**ntention to embody "Spirit-led" like Jesus, "who through the eternal Spirit offered Himself without blemish to God" (Hebrews 9:14). The same Holy Spirit who led Jesus in His humanity can lead us who share the same humanity!

> The Holy Spirit convicts us (John 16:7-11), regenerates us (Titus 3:5), seals us (Ephesians 1:13), sanctifies us (1 Corinthians 6:11), indwells us (1 Corinthians 3:16), and gives us assurance of salvation (Romans 8:16). As our Helper (John 14:16), the Holy Spirit teaches us (John 14:26), comforts us (Acts 9:31), leads us (Acts 11:12), strengthens us (Ephesians 3:16), provides for us (Philippians 1:19), empowers us (Acts 1:8), intercedes for us (Romans 8:26), and guides us into all truth (John 16:13). (See *Transforming Beliefs*, page 78)

While we journey through the labyrinth of life, let's engage in the **M**eans of grace available to us. "There isn't a single thing that Jesus said that we cannot do. There isn't a single thing that [H]e said that we can do on our own, but we are not on our own." (*Living in Christ's Presence*, page 116)

> How do we grieve the Holy Spirit? Since He is "the Spirit of truth" (John 14:17), anything that is false, deceitful, or hypocritical grieves Him. Since He is "the Spirit of grace" (Hebrews 10:29), anything that is revengeful, unforgiving, or unloving grieves Him. And since He is "the Spirit of holiness" (Romans 1:4), anything that is profane, heretical, or sinful grieves Him. (See *Transforming Beliefs*, page 80)

♫ Spirit of the living God, fall afresh on me . . . ♫

Reflecting on the Labyrinth of Leadership

RobbinsNest Ministries
Stop. Look. Listen.

TABLE FELLOWSHIP

"Thou dost prepare a table before me" (Psalm 23:5).

Although religious systems often prioritize dogmas and rules of order that keep outsiders outside, RobbinsNest thinks that table fellowship, as seen in Jesus *the* pastor, will be deliberate in us because the law of love repositions us to pay attention to and break bread with our "neighbor."

While we journey through the labyrinth of life, let's expand our **V**ision of Christ's table fellowship. FYI: It labeled Him "a glutton and a drunkard, a friend of tax collectors and sinners" (Luke 7:34).

Ten Examples of Table Fellowship in the Gospel According to Luke

1. Luke 5:29-39 (big reception at Levi's house)
2. Luke 7:36-50 (sinful lady at Simon's house)
3. Luke 9:10-17 (feeding of the 5000)
4. Luke 10:38-42 (Mary & Martha)
5. Luke 11:37-54 (unwashed hands & six woes)
6. Luke 14:1-14 (Sabbath healing & lesson)
7. Luke 15:1-2 (tax-gatherers & sinners)
8. Luke 19:1-10 (house guest of Zaccheus)
9. Luke 22:14-20 (the Lord's Supper)
10. Luke 24:13-43 (road to Emmaus & back)

While we journey through the labyrinth of life, let's build our **I**ntention to have table fellowship be deliberate in us. "Will you be eating this in your car?" "No, I will be sharing it with others."

We do more than "say grace" at table fellowship. We "DO [extend] grace." We position others and ourselves to see God acting in our lives to bring about what we cannot accomplish on our own.

Pastor, would you "DO grace" for us?   ○ Yes   ○ No   ○ Let's let someone else have a turn.

LOVE
(George Herbert, 1593–1633)

Love bade me welcome. Yet my soul drew back
    Guilty of dust and sin.
But quick-eyed Love, observing me grow slack
    From my first entrance in,
Drew nearer to me, sweetly questioning,
    If I lacked any thing.

A guest, I answered, worthy to be here:
    Love said, You shall be he.
I the unkind, ungrateful? Ah my dear,
    I cannot look on thee.
Love took my hand, and smiling did reply,
    Who made the eyes but I?

Truth Lord, but I have marred them: let my shame
    Go where it doth deserve.
And know you not, says Love, who bore the blame?
    My dear, then I will serve.
You must sit down, says Love, and taste my meat:
    So I did sit and eat.

While we journey through the labyrinth of life, let's engage in the **M**eans of grace for grace transfers us from the tabernacle to the TABLE in the wilderness!

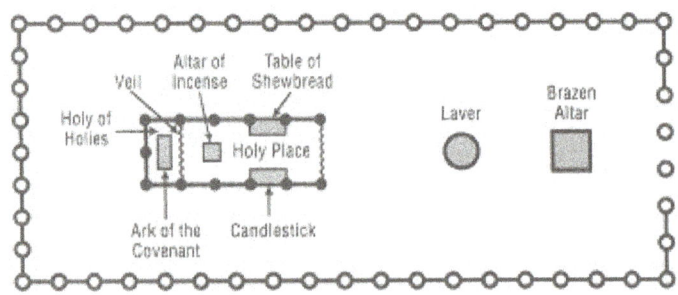

"This hope [of direct access to God in Christ] we have as an anchor of the soul, a hope both sure and steadfast and one which *enters within the veil*" (Heb. 6:19). In TABLE FELLOWSHIP we extend this hope to others—just as it is extended to us at the "already" Lord's Supper and at the "not yet" heavenly banquet.

Reflecting on the Labyrinth of Leadership

BE

"In Him we live and move and exist [have our being]" (Acts 17:28).

Although conferences help you DO things like "develop your brand" and "determine your price," RobbinsNest thinks that faithful pastors are first and foremost called to BE things like "in Christ" because only from this reality can one journey through this life and the next and bear good fruit.

While we journey through the labyrinth of life, let's expand our **V**ision of what it means to BE Christ formed. Celebrating the image of God established in us, we join in the sweet society of the Godhead and bring to our churches and world the persons we become (for this is what they see).

At the core of existence are Father and Son and Holy Spirit, not protons or neutrons or quarks. The reality from which our being and all other realities are derived from is the Holy Trinity.

While we journey through the labyrinth of life, let's build our **I**ntention to BE Christ formed. Instead of living as if we are what we achieve, what others say about us, and what we have, let us decide to abide in Christ and—from this position—bear fruit and have His joy made full in us.

Listed on our "To BE List" should be "Mary." Of course, both sisters—Mary and Martha—are present and accounted for in the Kingdom; nonetheless let us be "the good part" (Luke 10:38-42).

While we journey through the labyrinth of life, let's engage in the **M**eans of grace to BE Christ formed. While we "do" train (not try) for godliness (1 Timothy 4:7), we recognize that it's God who works in our lives bringing about what we don't deserve and can't accomplish on our own.

In "the easy yoke" we learn to BE, and then, as Dallas Willard says, "[W]e just observe the results. We don't make it happen. The burden is not ours. The Lord will take care of it, and we have to get out of [H]is way and stop messing with the things that we should leave to [H]is care. Then we will see the result, and we will know the reality of the easy yoke. And we will live with joy and power where we are, for now and for the future." (*Living in Christ's Presence*, 70-71)

B.E. [Blue Egg] Pastors Spiritual Exercise

Meditate on the following five sentences, focusing especially on the last word(s). Hear God say to you:

- Be still and know that I am *God*.
- Be still and know that *I am*.
- Be still and *know*.
- Be *still*.
- *Be*.

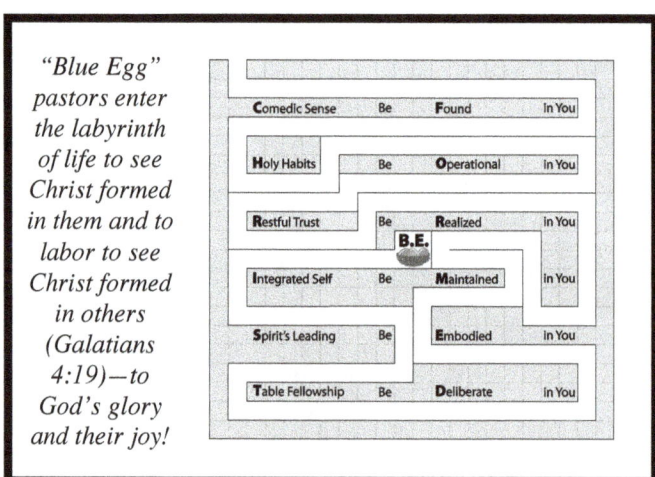

"Blue Egg" pastors enter the labyrinth of life to see Christ formed in them and to labor to see Christ formed in others (Galatians 4:19)—to God's glory and their joy!

Reflecting on the Labyrinth of Leadership

The following eight handouts focus on the framework for building leaders that Jesus constructs in His "Upper Room Discourse." The acrostic of "S.c.a.f.f.o.l.d." will help guide you through this section of the labyrinth of leadership.

Use the "Reflecting on the Labyrinth of Leadership" pages to record your thoughts and experiences around the Vision-Intention-Means pattern for spiritual formation. Feel free to use some space to doodle, too.

*Take note that the entire "Upper Room Discourse" text (John 13-17) is included in the Appendix.

SCAFFOLD FOR BUILDING LEADERS

Although a plethora of advice (books, webinars, conferences, etc.) bombards emerging leaders, RobbinsNest thinks Jesus' Upper Room Discourse offers the greatest leadership advice bar none because in it He—the greatest leader ever to live—constructs the framework for building leaders.

In His *Upper Room Discourse*—knowing that He was about to die, defeat death, and depart—Jesus constructs the S.C.A.F.F.O.L.D. (supporting framework) needed to build kingdom leaders.

S.C.A.F.F.O.L.D. supports us and positions us to work on kingdom projects beyond our natural reach. Jesus lays out the spiritual materials needed to form a structure from which to build leaders.

Jesus delivers the Upper Room Discourse in *John 13–17*. He presents within these five chapters a leadership-training seminar that the world would never offer and yet so desperately needs.

J. Oswald Sanders describes the Upper Room Discourse as Jesus' "*graduation address*" to the disciples (*Spiritual Leadership*, 51), His parting instruction on the essential qualities of leadership.

By using the following *chiastic structure* for the Upper Room Discourse, we realize and emphasize that the central element for building kingdom leaders is fruit-bearing friends of Jesus.

So what does Jesus say to His disciples, *His friends*? What does He want to make sure they get? What does He so much want them to remember as He goes and as they go forth to do His will?

1a **S**ervice to Others (13:1-20)
2a **C**onfront with Care (13:21–14:15)
3a **A**bide in Christ (14:16–15:11)
✝ **F**ruit-bearing **FRIEND** of Jesus (15:12-17)
3b **O**utcast in World (15:18–16:11)
2b **L**isten with Care (16:12-33)
1b **D**evotion to God (17:1-26)

Spiritual Exercise: Imagine yourself there in the Upper Room as you or someone else reads out loud John 13–17. Reflect on these crucial words of Jesus as you hear them spoken in one sitting.

Reflecting on the Labyrinth of Leadership

SERVICE TO OTHERS
—JOHN 13:1-20—

Jesus speaking: (14) "If I then, the Lord and the Teacher, washed your feet, you also ought to wash one another's feet. (15) For I gave you an example that you also should do as I did to you."

Although titles, degrees, and honors have their place in the pastorate, RobbinsNest thinks humble service to others makes a kingdom leader because *the* Pastor-Leader "did not come to be served, but to serve" (Matt. 20:28) and "emptied Himself, taking the form of a bond-servant" (Phil. 2:7).

VISION

A clear and vivid understanding of the goodness and desirability of (a) building service to others into the framework of ministry, (b) magnifying the office of pastor with humility, (c) laying aside selfish ambition, and (d) serving others because Jesus has first served us (cf. 1 John 4:10-11).

> *"Have this attitude in yourselves which was also in Christ Jesus, who . . . emptied Himself, taking the form of a bond-servant" (Philippians 2:5-7).*

INTENTION

A settled resolve to become more and more the kind of pastor who (a) can't care less about name recognition and who gets the credit, (b) does not have to sit at the head table, (c) says "Let's do it" more than "You do it," (d) intentionally listens to and blesses others, and (e) can wash others' feet.

> *"The Son of Man did not come to be served, but to serve, and to give His life a ransom for many" (Matthew 20:28).*

MEANS

Particular activities that can help one fulfill the above intention that's based on the vision of "service to others" include (a) reflecting on John 13:1-20, (b) writing a "help wanted ad" for a servant-leader, (c) engaging in S.E.R.V.I.C.E., and (d) reading meditatively Matthew 20:20-28.

> *"The church needs saints and servants, not 'leaders,' and if we forget the priority of service, the entire idea of leadership training becomes dangerous. Leadership training must still follow the pattern our Lord used with His twelve."*
>
> *— J Oswald Sanders, Spiritual Leadership, 148*

The following acrostic describes practical ways to build S.E.R.V.I.C.E. into kingdom leaders.

- **S**imple acts of kindness
- **E**ncouragement and edification
- **R**eceiving service with humility
- **V**oyaging with others through valleys
- **I**ntercessory prayer
- **C**ommon courtesies
- **E**ar for listening

Reflecting on the Labyrinth of Leadership

Confront with Care
— John 13:21–14:15 —

Jesus confronts His disciples with care: "Truly, truly, I say to you, that one of you will betray Me" (13:21). "Have I been so long with you, and yet you have not come to know Me, Philip?" (14:9).

Although many in leadership justify meanness and act as if it is better to be right than to be good, RobbinsNest thinks kingdom leaders will confront with care and progressively become like Jesus (who was/is right and good) because they are role models of holiness and loyal to truth and love.

Vision

A clear and vivid understanding of the goodness and desirability of (a) building "care-fronting" into the framework of ministry, (b) magnifying the office of pastor with truth and love, and (c) laying aside the ever-burdening weight of having to get your own way, get even, and get ahead.

"Grace, mercy and peace will be with us, from God the Father and from Jesus Christ, the Son of the Father, in truth and love" (2 John 3).

Intention

A settled resolve to become more and more the kind of pastor who confronts with care (a) apathy and inattention to commitments, (b) betrayal and the breaking of a confidence, (c) criticism and blame, (d) disputes and anger, etc.—and all this with fellow kingdom leaders and, too, the laity.

"Speaking the truth in love" (Ephesians 4:15).

Means

Particular activities that can help one fulfill the above intention that's based on the vision of "confront with care" include (a) reflecting on John 13:21–14:15, (b) observing the "rules for fair fighting," and (c) reading meditatively Matthew 18:15-17 and pondering how you can apply it.

Rules for Fair Fighting

- Stick to one issue, and don't bring up the past.
- Never say "never" or "always." ("You never listen to what I'm saying." "That's because you never express anything worth listening to.")
- Use "I feel . . ." statements. ("I feel like you are not listening to me." "I feel like you did not try to help." "I felt hurt when you did that.")
- Don't hit below the belt or use verbal harpoons. ("Shut up and listen to me." "Can't you do anything right?" "Who do you think you are?")
- Be open and honest and don't play games. ("I guess it's all my fault." "I guess I just can't do anything right." "What's wrong? *Nothing.*")
- Don't laugh or say, "You're kidding, right?" Also, choose the right time and right place, and don't quit before some resolution is reached.

TRANSFORMING PASTORS

Reflecting on the Labyrinth of Leadership

ABIDE IN CHRIST
—JOHN 14:16–15:11—

As He builds kingdom leaders, Jesus states, "I am the vine, you are the branches; he who abides in Me and I in him, he bears much fruit, for apart from Me you can do nothing" (John 15:5).

Although private enterprise and "pull-yourself-up-by-the-bootstraps" philosophy has its place in this world, RobbinsNest thinks that true kingdom leaders abide in Christ and submit to His word and will because, in the kingdom of God, they work in a power that is not their own or natural.

VISION

A clear and vivid understanding of the goodness and desirability of being (a) united in and at home in Christ and His body, the church, (b) led by and taught by the Holy Spirit, "the Spirit of truth," and (c) loved by and commanded by God the Father Almighty, maker of heaven and earth.

"Go therefore & make disciples of all the nations, baptizing them in the name [immersing them in the Trinitarian presence] of the Father & the Son & the Holy Spirit, teaching them to obey all that I commanded you; & lo, I am with you always, even to the end of the age" (Matt. 28:19-20).

INTENTION

A settled resolve to become more and more the kind of pastor who enjoys an ongoing, interactive, ever-deepening relationship with the Holy Trinity.

"Until Christ is formed in you" (Galatians 4:19).

MEANS

Particular activities that can help one be in a better position to fulfill the above intention that is based on the vision of "abide in Christ" include:

(a) Read and reflect on the poem entitled "Aaron" and consider writing a poem on abiding in Christ.

(b) Choose one commandment this week to obey completely, cheerfully, and without hesitation.

(c) Gaze upon a vine or tree and its branches and ponder Jesus' "apart from Me you can do nothing."

(d) Treasure what it means to be "In Christ"—e.g.,

- "we have redemption, the forgiveness of sin"

- "there is therefore now no condemnation"

- "we [His ποίημα] are created for good works"

AARON
by George Herbert (1593-1633) in *The Temple*

Holiness on the head,
Light and perfections on the breast,
Harmonious bells below, raising the dead
To lead them unto life and rest.
Thus are true Aarons drest.

Profaneness in my head,
Defects and darkness in my breast,
A noise of passions ringing me for dead
Unto a place where is no rest.
Poor priest thus am I drest.

Only another head
I have, another heart and breast,
Another music, making live not dead,
Without whom I could have no rest:
In him I am well drest.

Christ is my only head,
My alone only heart and breast,
My only music, striking me ev'n dead;
That to the old man I may rest,
And be in him new drest.

So holy in my head,
Perfect and light in my dear breast,
My doctrine tun'd by Christ, (who is not dead,
But lives in me while I do rest)
Come people; Aaron's drest.

Reflecting on the Labyrinth of Leadership

Fruit-Bearing Friend of Jesus
—John 15:12-17—

"I have called you friends, for all things that I have heard from My Father I have made known to you. You did not choose Me but I chose you, & appointed you that you would go & bear fruit."

Although innovative and efficient techniques and irrefutable laws may build corporate leaders, RobbinsNest thinks the central material needed for building kingdom leaders is a *fruit-bearing friend of Jesus* because apart from Him we can do nothing that bears good and lasting fruit.

Vision

A clear and vivid understanding of the goodness and desirability of (a) living within the holy Friendship of the Trinity, (b) recognizing the voice of the Father, (c) taking on the easy yoke of the Son, (d) bearing the fruit of the Spirit, and (e) doing this with the company of His friends.

A friend of Jesus said, "But the fruit of the Spirit is love, joy, peace, patience, kindness, goodness, faithfulness, gentleness, self-control; against such things there is no law" (Galatians 5:22, 23).

Can you see your Friend laughing and playing? Do you plan to laugh and play with your Friend? How would He laugh and play if He were you?

Intention

A settled resolve to become more and more the kind of pastor who (a) talks with Jesus, (b) befriends His friends, (c) shares His stories, & (d) trusts His leading.

"Behold, I stand at the door and knock; if anyone hears My voice & opens the door, I will come in to him, & will dine with him, & he with Me" (Revelation 3:20).

Means

Particular activities that can help one fulfill the above intention that's based on the vision of being a "fruit-bearing friend of Jesus" include these transforming habits:

Fellowship. Come alongside "His friends" for mutual support and accountability. [Note: 70% of pastors say they do not have a close friend in or outside the church.]

Prayer. Carry on a conversation with your Friend throughout the day about matters that matter to you both. Share your stories, secrets, and struggles. Stay real and open.

Reflecting on the Labyrinth of Leadership

RobbinsNest Ministries

OUTCAST IN **W**ORLD
—JOHN 15:18–16:11—

Jesus says to His not-of-the-world disciples, "They will make you outcasts from the synagogue, but an hour is coming for everyone who kills you to think that he is offering service to God" (16:2).

Although this dog-eat-dog world awards ambitious people who make a name for themselves, RobbinsNest thinks kingdom leaders are built by a contrasting and forward thinking worldview because they, like their Lord, sojourn as outcasts in this world with eternity in their hearts.

VISION

A clear and vivid understanding of the goodness and desirability of (a) a paradigm shift from geocentric (earth is the center) to theocentric (God is the center) and ~~helio~~ huioscentric (everything revolves around the *Son*!), and (b) while a pilgrim on earth, training to reign with God in eternity.

"I [Jesus] have given them Your word; and the world has hated them, because they are not of the world, even as I am not of the world. I do not ask You to take them out of the world, but to keep them from the evil one. They are not of the world, even as I am not of the world" (John 17:14-16).

INTENTION

A settled resolve to become more and more the kind of pastor who is at peace with the fact that (a) true discipleship will not mean greater popularity in this fallen world, and (b) he must, as "an alien and stranger, abstain from fleshly lusts, which wage war against the soul" (1 Peter 2:11).

"All these [OT kingdom leaders] died in faith, . . . having confessed that they were strangers and exiles on the earth. . . . They desire a better country, that is, a heavenly one. Therefore God is not ashamed to be called their God; for He has prepared a city for them" (Hebrews 11:13-16).

MEANS

Particular activities that can help one fulfill the above intention that's based on the vision of being an "outcast in world" leader include (a) reflecting on John 15:18–16:11, (b) pondering the questions below, and (c) exercising the transforming habits of secrecy, frugality, and evangelism.

Questions to Ponder

❶ How could Jesus be an outcast in the world that He made?
❷ Why is the Holy Spirit found a lot in the S.C.A.F.F.O.L.D.?
❸ What does it mean for us to be in the world but not of it?

❹ True or False:
When relevance trumps reverence, of-this-world leaders experiment with their churches and end up doing whatever the world can do but a decade later and worse (e.g., "Sunday School Musical").

Reflecting on the Labyrinth of Leadership

LISTEN WITH CARE
—JOHN 16:12-33—

"I have many more things to say to you, but you cannot bear them now. But when He, the Spirit of truth, comes, He will guide you into all the truth; for He will not speak on His own initiative, but whatever He hears, He will speak; and He will disclose to you what is to come" (John 16:12, 13).

Although modernity purports that God is either dead or too busy or detached to care or relate to us, RobbinsNest thinks we are wise to listen with care for God to speak and communicate with us because He is not only alive, but He has given us life so that we may have fellowship with Him.

VISION

A clear and vivid understanding of the goodness and desirability of recognizing the voice of God in (a) the written Word soundly interpreted by the historic church, (b) the still small voice inwardly impressed by the Holy Spirit, and (c) the earthly events guided by our heavenly Father.

"Truly, truly, I say to you, . . ."

INTENTION

A settled resolve to become more and more the kind of pastor who is willing and able to (a) set aside regular times to "stop, look, listen" to the Triune God, (b) notice God's "footprints"—His movement and activity—and how He relates to mankind, and (c) be at peace when God is silent.

"This is My beloved Son, with whom I am well-pleased; listen to Him" (Matthew 17:5).

MEANS

Particular activities that can help one fulfill the above intention that is based on the vision to "listen with care" include (a) having a *minute of silence* at the end of a meal in a restaurant, (b) having a *meal in silence* with family and/or friends, and (c) creating space and time to L.I.S.T.E.N.:

> *Leave.* We intentionally postpone noise and retire from the rat race. We turn off our cell phones, radios, televisions, and other technologies that surround us with sound.
>
> *Invoke.* We welcome God's presence, and we call upon Him to initiate a wordless conversation—a meeting where "the Spirit Himself bears witness with our spirit."
>
> *Surrender.* We abandon outcomes to God. We withdraw from using words to manage our worlds and reputations. We relax our grip on the need to make things happen.
>
> *Trust.* We believe that "The Lord will fight for [us] while [we] keep silent" (Exodus 14:14) and that God "acts in behalf of the one who waits for Him" (Isaiah 64:4).
>
> *Exist.* We become the kind of people who can be alive, real, and with God in silence. We know He is God and that "in Him we live and move and exist" (Acts 17:28).
>
> *Notice.* We focus our attention on God. We "stop, look, listen" to His movement and activity. We pay attention to how God is writing His-story on the pages of our lives.

Reflecting on the Labyrinth of Leadership

RobbinsNest Ministries
Stop. Look. Listen.

DEVOTION TO GOD
—JOHN 17:1-26—

"And lifting up His eyes to heaven, [Jesus] said, "Father . . ." (John 17:1).

Although pushy marketeers and personalities may turn around plateau or declining churches, RobbinsNest thinks that Jesuslike prayer and devotion to God builds God-glorifying churches because the kingdom of God, in which *the* Church resides, is born from above, not manmade.

VISION

A clear and vivid understanding of the goodness and desirability of (a) building kingdom leaders with God-like love, (b) knowing rationally and empirically the gloriously joyous love within the Godhead, and (c) imaging forth the essential and distinguishing qualities of kingdom leadership.

"The love with which You loved Me may be in them, & I in them" (John 17:26).

INTENTION

A settled resolve to become more and more the kind of pastor who, like Jesus, (a) prays for himself (vv. 1-5), his disciples/leaders (vv. 6-19), and future disciples/leaders (vv. 20-26), (b) banks on the Father to answer, and (c) goes forth to do his part, including taking up his cross.

"This is eternal life, that they may know You, the only true God" (John 17:3).

MEANS

Particular activities that can help one fulfill the above intention that is based on the vision of "devotion to God" include (a) praying for what Jesus prayed for, (b) training to live out what Jesus prayed for, and (c) pondering how S.C.A.F.F.O.L.D. is found in Jesus' high priestly prayer.

The Road ("ROUTE 66") of Transformation

6 Petitions of Jesus (1 for Himself and 5 for His disciples). He prays for:
1. His *Glorification*—"Glorify Thy Son" (vv. 1, 5)
2. Our *Protection*—"Keep them in Thy name / from the evil one" (vv. 11, 15)
3. Our *Joy*—"That they may have My joy made full in themselves" (v. 13)
4. Our *Sanctification*—"Sanctify them in the truth" (v. 17)
5. Our *Unity*—"That they may all be one" (vv. 20-23)
6. Our *Destiny*—"That they . . . be with Me where I am" (v. 24)

6 Marks of the Church (distinguishing features). The church is evidenced by:
1. Obedience—"They have kept Thy word" (v. 6)
2. Joy—"That they may have My joy made full in themselves" (v. 13)
3. Holiness—"They are not of this world" (v. 14)
4. Mission—"I also have sent them into the world" (v. 18)
5. Unity—"That they may be perfected in unity" (v. 23)
6. Love—"The love wherewith Thou didst love Me may be in them" (v. 26)

Reflecting on the Labyrinth of Leadership

The following eight handouts focus on the core values of RobbinsNest and conceivably of your ministry, too. The acrostic of "C.o.m.p.a.s.s." will help guide you through this section of the labyrinth of leadership.

Begin to write your answers to the handouts' questions on the lines provided, and then continue to write on the "Reflecting on the Labyrinth of Leadership" pages. Go ahead, put on your "creative cap" and doodle ideas, images, and even an acrostic!

Take note that help for how to "Write Your Own Eulogy" (plus an example) is included in the Appendix.

CORE VALUES

Although today's "image-is-everything" baits us to create brands and live mile-wide, inch-deep lives, RobbinsNest thinks pastors and churches are to be faithful to their calling with core values intact and intentional because the Christian life is deep and weighty and for the glory of God.

Citizens (contrasted to tourists) of God's kingdom don't live by clichés, sound bites, and slogans. They think. They think hard, long, and often. Reason and logic are their companions on the Way. They have knowledge and truth, not mere opinions and traditions, as they journey through life.

RobbinsNest Ministries holds on to core values as it navigates through the course of transition and into the future of service. These guiding principles form the C.O.M.P.A.S.S. that directs and motivates the content and scheduling of all domestic and international ministries of RobbinsNest.

Jesus Christ is at the center of RobbinsNest. "Jesus is Lord" establishes and unifies the mission and message. To God's glory and our joy, RobbinsNest's beliefs and practices are anchored to Scripture and rooted in church history. As it reaches out to pastors and small churches around the world, the ministry makes itself mobile and affordable. Going to where they are, it presents a reliable pattern for spiritual formation. In all that it does (e.g., the nurturing, small groups, events, and writing), RobbinsNest (1) focuses and expands their vision of the goodness and desirability of Christ being formed in them, (2) builds up their intention to be the kinds of people who routinely and naturally develop an ongoing, interactive, ever-deepening relationship with Jesus, and (3) engages them in the means of spiritual disciplines on the road of transformation.

What are your core values? What would be a part of your compass? Begin a list of guiding principles that inform and influence who you are and what you do inside and outside the church.

Reflecting on the Labyrinth of Leadership

CHRIST-CENTERED

Jesus said to [Thomas and to the rest of the disciples], "I am the way [to God], and the truth [about God], and the life [with God]; no one comes to the Father, but through Me" (John 14:6).

Although a cultural shift toward "tolerance" and "change" evolves, RobbinsNest thinks Christ-Centeredness is a core value to uphold because "Jesus Christ is Lord" was the church's earliest confession (Philippians 2:11), continues to be true today, and will forever be what actually is so.

Christ-Centered indicates:

- My teaching focuses on the Lord's teaching (e.g., the Sermon on the Mount) and life (e.g., the Gospels).
- My life moves toward becoming the kind of person that has an ongoing, interactive rapport with Christ.
- My marriage/family has Jesus Christ as the head of the house, the unseen Guest at every meal, vacation, etc.
- My church lifts up (not takes down) the cross of Christ, and it partakes of (not puts off) the Lord's Supper.
- My theology embraces *Solus Christus*, that is, through Christ alone one is saved and has a mediator to God.
- My ministry and mission unites with Christ's ministry and mission for this planet (e.g., Matthew 28:18ff.).

- _____

_____ ☺

"What we want, if men become Christians at all, is to keep them in the state of mind I call 'Christianity And'. You know—Christianity and the Crisis, Christianity and the New Psychology, Christianity and the New Order, Christianity and Faith Healing, Christianity and Psychical Research, Christianity and Vegetarianism, Christianity and Spelling Reform. If they must be Christians, let them at least be Christians with a difference. Substitute for the faith itself some Fashion with a Christian colouring. Work on their horror of the Same Old Thing."

(Uncle Screwtape, Letter 25)

Question: What might Uncle Screwtape include today in his "Christianity And" examples?

_____

Naming Our Core Values

- Would you consider "Christ-Centered" a core value?   ○ Yes   ○ No   ○ I am not sure
- If "Yes," then how does one see this core value demonstrated in your life and ministry?

_____

Christ-Centered Idea ⊃ Place an empty chair at the meal table, in front of the TV, etc. for Christ.

Reflecting on the Labyrinth of Leadership

ORTHODOXY/ORTHOPRAXY

Paul, with his apprentice Timothy, wrote, "As you therefore have received Christ Jesus the Lord, so walk in Him, having been firmly rooted and now being built up in Him and established in your faith, just as you were instructed, and overflowing with gratitude" (Colossians 2:6, 7).

Although a flippant fascination with "new and improved" stirs the economy, RobbinsNest thinks orthodoxy and orthopraxy—two sides of the same *koinonia*—form a core value to treasure because established right belief and practice unite the communion of saints, both past and present.

Orthodoxy	Orthopraxy
Right Belief	Right Behavior
Historic Creeds	Present Deeds
Christian Content	Christian Conduct
Actual Knowledge	Actual Godliness
Driven by *Vera Deus*	Driven by *Vera Homo*
"Obedient to the faith" (Acts 6:7)	"The obedience of faith" (Romans 1:5)
The Contemplative Life: Love God	The Active Life: Love Neighbor

Orthodoxy and orthopraxy unite the people of God from the inside out. "The faith which was once for all delivered to the saints" (Jude 3) yokes us together with Christ to "follow in His steps" (1 Peter 2:21). We witness these two become one core value in (a) the Lord's Supper, (b) the Lord's Prayer, and (c) believer's baptism. What God has joined together, let no "ism" separate.

> This unifying value also divides. "Come out from their midst and be separate" (2 Corinthians 6:17). In His Upper Room Discourse, Jesus said to His disciples, "If you were of the world, the world would love its own; but because you are not of the world, but I chose you out of the world, therefore the world hates you" (John 15:19; cf. Jesus' High Priestly Prayer in 17:14ff.).
>
> *Why does* Orthodoxy/Orthopraxy *separate the church from the world, the sheep from the goats?*

Naming Our Core Values

- Would you consider "Orthodoxy/Orthopraxy" a core value? ○ Yes ○ No ○ I am not sure
- If "Yes," then how does one see this core value demonstrated in your life and ministry?

Orthodoxy/Orthopraxy Idea ⇒ To help you live from the inside out, do the following In-N-Out spiritual exercise. Order a "Double-Double" this week, that is, (1) spend *two* hours in solitude paying attention to God and to His holy Word, and (2) do *two* random, unselfish acts of kindness.

Reflecting on the Labyrinth of Leadership

Mobile/*Missio Regni Dei*

Jesus said to His disciples, "Go therefore and make disciples of all the nations, baptizing them in the name of the Father and the Son and the Holy Spirit, teaching them to obey all that I commanded you; and lo, I am with you always, even to the end of the age" (Matthew 28:19, 20).

Although pastors and church members are often appraised and praised by how much time they spend at the church, RobbinsNest thinks optimal ministry is mobile because God's kingdom mission for us (the *missio regni Dei*) is to "Go" forth and invite people into a life with God.

Of course "not forsaking our own assembling together, as is the habit of some" (Hebrews 10:25), let us, like Jesus, be portable and serve the world around us as we go about our daily lives. Why be mobile and global? Because "the Lord your God is with you wherever you go" (Joshua 1:9).

A shout out for long pastorates! God's kingdom mission for pastors is not to climb the corporate ladder, nor leave when the sheep bite. Mobile does not mean "run away, escape responsibilities." Pastors who make long-term investments more often yield higher dividends than clergy day traders.

Expectations! They can be spoken or unspoken, written or unwritten, official or unofficial. (E.g., How many hours are you to be at church per week? How much money are you to give?)

How does your church define a "good" pastor?

_____

_____

How do you define a "good" church member?

_____

_____

Naming Our Core Values

- Would you consider "Mobile/*Missio Regni Dei*" a core value? ○ Yes ○ No ○ I'm not sure
- If "Yes," then how does one see this core value demonstrated in your life and ministry?

_____

Mobile/*Missio Regni Dei* Idea ↪ During the following month, intentionally (1) plan to be away one night from church (that you normally would be at church) in order to serve the world around you (i.e., visit a shut-in, host a dinner for neighbors, volunteer at a charity, etc.), (2) encourage and recognize (privately and publically) others that do the same, and (3) memorize Joshua 1:9.

Reflecting on the Labyrinth of Leadership

PATH: VISION-INTENTION-MEANS

Regarding his spiritual formation, Paul stated, "I have been crucified with Christ; and it is no longer I who live, but Christ lives in me; and the life which I now live in the flesh I live by [faith in/the faith of] the Son of God, who loved me, and delivered Himself up for me" (Galatians 2:20).

Although cynicism is the present product produced by the plethora of programs promising the "key" for success, RobbinsNest thinks there is indeed a reliable path for spiritual formation because "Vision-Intention-Means" has proved to be fruitful, not faddish, for real transformation.

Pastors (1) focus and expand our *vision* of the goodness and desirability of Christ being formed in us, (2) build up our *intention* to be the kinds of people who routinely and naturally develop an ongoing, interactive relationship with Jesus, and (3) engage us in the *means* of spiritual disciplines.

VISION: PASTORS DEVELOP A CLEAR AND VIVID UNDERSTANDING OF THE GOODNESS AND DESIRABILITY OF SPIRITUAL GROWTH FOR THEMSELVES (ALONG WITH THE GROWTH OF THEIR PEOPLE).

The Default Gospel
- Great Diagnostic Question: "Suppose that you were to die tonight and stand before God and He were to say to you, 'Why should I let you into My heaven?' What would you say?"
- Great Response to the Question: What if I do not die tonight? Is there a gospel for me?

INTENTION: PASTORS DECIDE AND MAKE A SETTLED RESOLVE TO ADVANCE IN THEIR OWN SPIRITUAL FORMATION (ALONG WITH THE SPIRITUAL FORMATION OF THEIR CONGREGATIONS).

Holy Rhythm of Life
- Great Questions: What kind of person do you aim and plan to become? Is it possible for your spirit *and* flesh to be willing and strong to do God's will on earth, as it is in heaven?
- Great Exercise: Write your own eulogy (see pages 128 and 129 for help and an example).

MEANS: PASTORS INSTITUTE PARTICULAR ACTIVITIES AND ARRANGEMENTS THAT ARE SUITED TO CARRY THEIR OWN (AND THEIR CONGREGANTS') INTENTION INTO THE REALITY OF THEIR VISION.

As Was His Custom
- Great Truth: "For we do not have a high priest who cannot sympathize with our weaknesses, but one who has been tempted in all things as we are, yet without sin" (Hebrews 4:15).
- Great Follow-up Question: How could Jesus have been tempted like us, and yet not sin?

Naming Our Core Values

- Would you consider the "V.I.M. Path" a core value?   ◯ Yes   ◯ No   ◯ I am not sure
- If "Yes," then how does one see this core value demonstrated in your life and ministry?

Path: V.I.M. Idea ⊃ Reflect on and answer the questions found on this handout. Share your thoughts with fellow pilgrims on the labyrinth of leadership. And do begin to write your eulogy!

Reflecting on the Labyrinth of Leadership

AFFORDABLE/ACCESSIBLE

Although consultants advise "Go for the market" and tout profit margins, RobbinsNest thinks kingdom goods and services should be, among other things, affordable and accessible because, as Jesus said, "It is more blessed to give than to receive" and "Freely you received, freely give."

Regarding goods and services, RobbinsNest uses "M.A.N.N.A. economics." So, "What is it?" ☺

- **M**ANAGE-ABILITY — *It's handling wisely, with discipline, God's kingdom resources.* Believing God supplies exactly what we need (just as He did for His people in the wilderness), we function, notwithstanding difficulties, with frugality and margins in place. (Cf. John Wesley's "earn-save-give . . . all you can" financial plan; plus Proverbs 30:8, 9)

- **A**FFORD-ABILITY — *It's making available the goods and services that God entrusts to us.* Believing God supplies generously what we need (just as He did for His people in the wilderness), we function, notwithstanding disparities, as ministers, not as merchants. (Cf. John Piper's "whatever you can afford" policy; plus Matthew 10:8; Acts 20:35)

- **N**O MERE-ABILITY — *It's relying daily on God's extraordinary ability to supply our needs.* Believing God supplies all-powerfully what we need (just as He did for His people in the wilderness), we function, notwithstanding displeasures, with divine *OMER*-like provisions. (Cf. John Bunyan's "pilgrim's progress"; plus Ephesians 3:20, 21; Philippians 4:19)

- **N**OTE-ABILITY — *It's acknowledging God as the prominent and notable hero in our story.* Believing God supplies independently what we need (just as He did for His people in the wilderness), we function, notwithstanding distinctions, as dependents on Jehovah-Jireh. (Cf. John Ortberg's "who is this man?" reputation and renown; plus Psalm 46:10, 11)

- **A**CCESS-ABILITY — *It's catering services by being portable, personable, and adaptable.* Believing God supplies befittingly what we need (just as He did for His people in the wilderness), we function, notwithstanding traditions, with intentionality and flexibility. (Cf. John the Baptist's "the kingdom of heaven is at hand" message; plus Matthew 5:1 ff.)

Just what did God do for His people in the wilderness?
(Match the following—See Exodus 16 for help!)

A. Manage-ability	____ The people weren't to horde; if they did, the manna became wormy.
B. Afford-ability	____ The people went out every morning to gather and cook their manna.
C. No mere-ability	____ The people didn't pay for the manna; it was free and not even taxed.
D. Note-ability	____ The people received the manna as they traveled in the wilderness.
E. Access-ability	____ The people would know the Lord is God (even "the Bread of Life").

Naming Our Core Values

- Would you consider "Affordable/Accessible" a core value? ○ Yes ○ No ○ I'm not sure
- If "Yes," then how does one see this core value demonstrated in your life and ministry?

_____

Affordable/Accessible Idea ⊃ Offer a resource to another pastor/church with no strings attached.

Reflecting on the Labyrinth of Leadership

SMALL CHURCHES

Jesus said, "For where two or three [note the simplicity of the church] have gathered together in My name, there I am [note the greatness of the church] in their midst" (Matthew 18:20).

Although church consultants often treat small churches as a problem that God wants to fix, RobbinsNest thinks they are a strategy God uses to bring about His kingdom purpose because they are consistent with how He has operated His divine conspiracy throughout holy history.

Consider God's "Small" Liking:

- God chose to have O Little Town of Bethlehem (Micah 5:2) as the birthplace of His Son.
- Jesus was raised in a small town. "Can any good thing come out of Nazareth?" (John 1:46).
- According to God, Gideon assembled too many soldiers, thus inviting pride (Judges 7:2).
- New Testament churches were largely small churches that congregated in private houses.
- God utilizes mustard seed size agents to accomplish His great cause (Matthew 13:31-33).

According to the National Congregations Study, 59% of the U.S. Protestant and other Christian churches have a weekly attendance of 99 or less, with the median U.S. church (i.e., half being smaller and half being larger) having 75 regular participants in worship on Sunday mornings.

Consider Our Churches' Liking:

- Do we count people because people count?
- Do we define success like God defines success?
- Do we force God's hand to take *it* to the next level?
- Do we secretly compete with the church down the street?
- Do we give thanks for and work with the people who are there?

Blessed are the large churches, too! With the *megas* already commanding resources and respect, RobbinsNest intentionally targets small churches (i.e., providing them and their pastors resources and respect). They are to be admired and esteemed, not patronized, felt sorry for, or lamented.

Naming Our Core Values

- Would you consider "Small Churches" a core value?   ○ Yes   ○ No   ○ I am not sure
- If "Yes," then how does one see this core value demonstrated in your life and ministry?

Small Churches Idea ⊃ Take some time to ponder the following "What ifs" and then write an encouraging letter or email to a small church pastor that you know (note that it can be yourself).

What if small churches are not a problem God wants to fix, but rather a strategy He wants to use?
What if small churches are not a setback to avoid, but rather a means of grace to uphold and bless?
What if small churches are not the achilles heel of God's kingdom, but rather the true backbone?

Reflecting on the Labyrinth of Leadership

RobbinsNest Ministries
Stop. Look. Listen.

Soli Deo Gloria

"Whether, then, you eat or drink or whatever you do, do all to the glory of God" (1 Cor. 10:31).

Although "God is dead" or at least irrelevant is peddled in the public square, RobbinsNest thinks "*Soli Deo Gloria*" is a core value to commend because this is a God-bathed, God-permeated world where He is the prime mover and sustainer, the most alive and relevant inhabitant and hero.

RobbinsNest affirms the five *sola* statements of the Protestant Reformation; and *Soli Deo Gloria* summarizes these *solas* that encapsulate the heart of biblical theology and the Christian faith.

1. *Sola Scriptura* (Scripture Alone)
   The Scriptures of the Old and New Testaments, given by divine inspiration, are God's Word, the only infallible rule of faith and practice. (2 Timothy 3:14-17; Matthew 5:17, 18)

2. *Solus Christus* (Christ Alone)
   Salvation is accomplished by the mediatory work of Christ alone. His sinless life and substitutionary death are sufficient for our redemption. (1 Timothy 2:5, 6; Galatians 2:20)

3. *Sola Gratia* (Salvation by Grace Alone)
   Salvation comes via God's grace alone, His acting in our lives to bring about what we do not deserve or merit and cannot accomplish on our own. (Ephesians 2:8, 9; Romans 3:24)

4. *Sola Fide* (Justification by Faith Alone)
   Faith alone in Christ alone brings justification, a legal act of God in which He forgives our sins and imputes Christ's righteousness to us. (Romans 5:1; 3:27; John 3:16)

5. *Soli Deo Gloria* (Glory to God Alone)
   Because salvation is of God and accomplished by God, it is ultimately for His glory alone, for His name's sake and the display of His holiness. (1 Corinthians 10:31; 1 Peter 4:11)

> **Isaiah 64:4**
>
> *God works . . .*
>
> - For us giving us faith
> - In us bearing fruit
> - Through us making disciples
>
> *as we wait for Him, that is, . . .*
>
> - Stop
> - Look
> - Listen
>
> *for Him—to His glory & our joy!*
>
>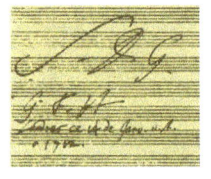

We say together, with one voice, "For Your glory, Lord, we live."

Naming Our Core Values

- Would you consider "*Soli Deo Gloria*" a core value?   ○ Yes   ○ No   ○ I am not sure
- If "Yes," then how does one see this core value demonstrated in your life and ministry?

Soli Deo Gloria Idea ⊃ (1) Like Bach/Handel, write "SDG" at the end of your sermon (masterpiece ☺). (2) Like Baxter/Spurgeon, catechize your people on "What is the chief end of man?".

Reflecting on the Labyrinth of Leadership

The following seven handouts focus on magnifying the office of pastor. The double acrostic of "P.a.s.t.o.r. S.k.e.t.c.h." will help guide you through this section of the labyrinth of leadership.

Do write on the handouts your answers to questions, as well as your questions to answer. And use the "Reflecting on the Labyrinth of Leadership" pages to take notes, record your involvement with the spiritual exercises, and, yes, doodle.

*Take note that a "Litany of Affirmation" for pastors is included in the Appendix.

MAGNIFY YOUR OFFICE

"I magnify my office" (Romans 11:13).

Although jokes about pastors are in vogue and many in and out of the church belittle their position, RobbinsNest thinks it is high time to magnify the office of pastor and to dignify their sacred call because they are shepherds of the very ones that God purchased with His own blood (Acts 20:28)!

If the Apostle Paul felt the need to say in his day, "I magnify my office" (Romans 11:13), then how much more do today's pastors need to do the same. The time has come to recover the significance of pastoral ministry and to dignify the call that God still extends to men and women.

Why has the office and service of the pastor been degraded and disgraced (i.e., de-magnified)? What happened to the esteem and worth? How did pastors loose their influence and "weight"?

_____

_____

What is a pastor? Following is a sketch, an outline of the chief features of the office. A pastor is a(n):

P.A.S.T.O.R. S.K.E.T.C.H.

Physician of the **S**oul
"I will remain and continue with you all for your progress and joy in the faith" (Philippians 1:25).

Administrator of the **K**eys
"I will give you the keys of the kingdom of heaven" (Matthew 16:19).

Shepherd of the **E**kklesia
"Shepherd the church of God which He purchased with His own blood" (Acts 20:28).

Teacher of the **T**ruth
"I will give you shepherds after My own heart, who will feed you on knowledge and understanding" (Jeremiah 3:15).

Overseer of the **C**hurch
"Be on guard for yourselves and for all the flock, among which the Holy Spirit has made you overseers" (Acts 20:28).

Role model of **H**oliness
"In all things show yourself to be an example of good deeds, with purity in doctrine, dignified, sound in speech which is beyond reproach" (Titus 2:7, 8).

What feature(s) would you emphasize as you sketch out the office of pastor? Would you add or subtract anything from the P.A.S.T.O.R. S.K.E.T.C.H. above? Finish the sentence: A pastor is . . .

_____

_____

Idea: Set your alarm for 11:13 a.m. When it goes off, give thanks to the Lord for being a pastor!

Reflecting on the Labyrinth of Leadership

RobbinsNest Ministries
Stop. Look. Listen.

PHYSICIAN OF THE SOUL

"I will remain and continue with you all for your progress and joy in the faith" (Philippians 1:25).

Although the pastoral office has been secularized and homogenized, debased and defined as running a church, RobbinsNest thinks the Puritans' term "physician of the soul" captures what a pastor is because a pastor looks out for the spiritual health of those entrusted to his care.

> Confronted early in his ministry by the secular and institutional responsibilities of modern pastoral identity, Eugene Peterson reflects, "I didn't like it and decided, after an interval of confused disorientation, that being a physician of the souls took priority over running a church, and that I would be guided in my pastoral vocation by wise predecessors rather than contemporaries." (*The Contemplative Pastor*, 67, 68)

****

"We must labour to be acquainted, not only with the persons, but with the state of all our people, with their inclinations and conversations; what are the sins of which they are most in danger, and what duties they are most apt to neglect, and what temptations they are most liable to; for if we know not their temperament or disease, we are not likely to prove successful physicians." (Richard Baxter, *The Reformed Pastor*, 90)

As physicians of the soul, pastors C.A.R.E. for their people. They . . .

Check over their condition (listen & observe)
Advise them of their state (w/ grace & reason)
Repair their V.I.M. (Vision, Intention, Means)
Evaluate & follow up on their progress & joy

Pastors . . .

Comfort the bereaved
Attend to the dying
Reassure the sick
Encourage all

Jesus stated to the scribes and Pharisees, "It is not those who are well who need a physician, but those who are sick. I have not come to call the righteous but sinners to repentance" (Luke 5:31, 32).

Diagnostic questions to ask for their progress and joy in the faith:

How do you see God writing His story on the pages of your life?
How has your vision of God expanded and gained focus?
How do you thirst for God and live as He intends?
What do you do with all your sin and guilt?
How do you get ready for Sundays?
What habits do you practice?

Idea for the Physician of the Soul ⊃ Visit your people in their homes and do a "home blessing" (Invoke, Intercede, Inspire). Think of this practice as a kind of annual checkup for the congregants.

Reflecting on the Labyrinth of Leadership

ADMINISTRATOR OF THE KEYS

"I will give you the keys of the kingdom of heaven" (Matthew 16:19).

Although "the pastor" increasingly depreciates into a figurehead, RobbinsNest thinks the pastor executes true power as an "administrator of the keys" because he opens and closes God's kingdom doors through preaching the gospel, administering the sacraments, and disciplining the church.

****

"I will give you the PIN number for the KEYP.A.D. of the kingdom."
(NASB—New Acrostic Steve Built ☺)

As an administrator of the keys, a pastor . . .

- **P**REACHES THE GOSPEL

    Pastors give the blessed welcome via God-glorifying, Christ-centered, Spirit-led preaching.

    Ask: Must Jesus rise from the dead for this sermon to work? Does it open up the gospel?

    Pastor:
    ⌕ Preach the gospel with boldness (the whole counsel of God, not the default gospel)
    —Acts 20:27—

- **A**DMINISTERS THE SACRAMENTS

    Pastors are in charge of the sacraments—the rites and services of the holy, universal church.

    You are the portal to "BE.COM": **B**aptism, **E**ucharist . **C**onfession, **O**rdination, **M**arriage

    Pastor:
    ⌕ Administer the sacraments with understanding ("What does this rite mean to you?")
    —Exodus 12:26—

- **D**ISCIPLINES THE CHURCH

    Pastors use the keys to open and close the doors to people's thoughts, attitudes, and actions.

    Use the "key" principle in Matthew 18 when you confront, correct, and excommunicate.

    Pastor:
    ⌕ Discipline the church with humility ("First take the log out of your own eye, . . .")
    —Matthew 7:5—

****

Peter, Paul, and other "pastors" used the keypad in the early church. As Frederick Dale Bruner explains, "Jews were ushered into the *ekklesia*, later the Samaritans, and still later gentiles, by apostles and others proclaiming Jesus as It. That is what the responsible preaching of the gospel (the administration of the keys) fundamentally is: sustained Christ-centeredness." Bruner continues then to explain the disciplinary understanding of the keypad: "Jesus gives the church the right to ban disobedient believers from ('bind') and to admit repentant believers to ('loose') the communion of the church." (*Matthew, Vol. 2, "The Churchbook: Matthew 13–28,"* page 577)

Reflecting on the Labyrinth of Leadership

SHEPHERD OF THE EKKLESIA

"Shepherd the church of God which He purchased with His own blood" (Acts 20:28).

Although the image of "shepherd" is viewed as pre-modern and even archaic, RobbinsNest thinks it remains a valid and useful metaphor to describe the contemporary pastor because a "pastor" (*poimen*) by definition leads, feeds, and cares for the ekklesia (i.e., God's called-out ones).

Today's pastor is called "Leader," "Reverend," "Minister," "Elder," "Preacher," as well as a few titles not so biblical or endearing (e.g., "Rancher," "Chaplain," "C.E.O.," "Entrepreneur," etc.).

Sheep pay a D.E.E.P. P.R.I.C.E. for "shepherds" (or are they butchers?) that are **D**ictatorial, **E**xploitive, **E**gotistical, **P**ompous, **P**ushy, **R**ejecting, **I**ntimidating, **C**oercive, and **E**ver-manipulative.

Idea for the Shepherd of the Ekklesia ⊃ Intentionally take time to (1) thank God for the sheep that are under your care, and (2) highlight the "pastoral prayer" in this week's worship service.

Ponder
(Answer – Explain – Discuss)

True or False: Having a MBA is more practical than having a MDiv in today's world for a pastor.

True or False: "Pastor" is the principal, unifying image of a congregational leader in the Bible.

True or False: The gift of pastor/shepherd is necessary for one who occupies the office of pastor.

True or False: Many who have the gift of pastor/shepherd do not occupy the office of pastor.

Compare & contrast the Good Shepherd (John 10; Psalm 23) with the bad shepherds (Ezekiel 34):

_____
_____
_____

Strike the shepherd and the sheep will scatter (bleat) . . . and the shepherd will suffer (bleed)!

Imagine
(Listen – Envision – Share)

The apostle Peter, the one who exhorts, "Shepherd the flock of God among you" (1 Peter 5:2), is the one whom Jesus confronts and restores in John 21:15-17.

****

(15) SO WHEN THEY HAD FINISHED BREAKFAST, JESUS SAID TO SIMON PETER, "SIMON, SON OF JOHN, DO YOU LOVE ME MORE THAN THESE?" HE SAID TO HIM, "YES, LORD; YOU KNOW THAT I LOVE YOU." HE SAID TO HIM, "TEND MY LAMBS." (16) HE SAID TO HIM AGAIN A SECOND TIME, "SIMON, SON OF JOHN, DO YOU LOVE ME?" HE SAID TO HIM, "YES, LORD; YOU KNOW THAT I LOVE YOU." HE SAID TO HIM, "SHEPHERD MY SHEEP." (17) HE SAID TO HIM THE THIRD TIME, "SIMON, SON OF JOHN, DO YOU LOVE ME?" PETER WAS GRIEVED BECAUSE HE SAID TO HIM THE THIRD TIME, "DO YOU LOVE ME?" AND HE SAID TO HIM, "LORD, YOU KNOW ALL THINGS; YOU KNOW THAT I LOVE YOU." JESUS SAID TO HIM, "TEND MY SHEEP."

Reflecting on the Labyrinth of Leadership

TEACHER OF THE TRUTH

*"I will give you shepherds after My own heart,
who will feed you on knowledge and understanding"* (Jeremiah 3:15).

Although academia relegates the Christian "faith" to the realm of treasured traditions, personal opinions, or blind commitments, RobbinsNest thinks pastors are "teachers of the truth" because they dwell in the knowledge of what actually is and bring that reality to others as God's spokesmen.

Modernity and its offspring, Post-modernity, would soon rather ignore or simply be indifferent to "kingdom pastors" as it meanders down Relativism Road, through the Tolerance Tunnel, and onward towards the two expanding and flourishing cities of Virtuous Doubt and Evolving Truth.

More so than all others, pastors are best positioned to be the teachers of the nations—to bring a worldview to the global table and answer Pilate's ageless question, "What is truth?" (John 18:38). To help people "know God and make Him known," pastors address life's persistent questions.

LIFE'S PERSISTENT QUESTIONS
(Small Group Discussion)

❶ *What is real?*
Truth is . . . the triune God and His kingdom

❷ *Who is blessed (well-off, successful)?*
Truth is . . . one who lives a with-God life

❸ *Who is a truly good person?*
Truth is . . . one pervaded with servant love

❹ *How does one become a truly good person?*
Truth is . . . surrender unto and follow Jesus

****

Is "orthodoxy" [established right belief]
- a working hypothesis to test?
- a premature conceit of certainty?
- a prejudice that shuns innovation?
- a product to be revised and enlarged?

> "The most important thing that is happening in your community is what is happening there under the administration of true pastors for Christ. If you, as a pastor, do not believe that, then you do not understand the dignity of what you are supposed to be doing. Whatever your situation, there is nothing more important on earth than to dwell in the knowledge of Christ and to bring that knowledge to others." (Dallas Willard, *Knowing Christ Today*, 211)
>
> *"This is eternal life, that they may know Thee, the only true God, and Jesus Christ whom Thou hast sent."*
> *(John 17:3)*

Idea for the Teacher of the Truth ⊃ The English word *catechize* comes from the Greek word *katecheo* meaning *to teach*. As a method to orderly instruct, use a catechism in an upcoming Bible study or sermon. Following is an example of the Question-Answer-Scripture format:

Question: How do we know there is a God? **Answer:** The light of nature in man, and the works of God, plainly declare that there is a God; but His word and Spirit only do effectually reveal Him unto us for our salvation. **Scripture:** *Romans 1:18-20; Psalm 19:1-2; 2 Timothy 3:15; 1 Corinthians 1:21-24; 2:9, 10; Matthew 11:27.*

Reflecting on the Labyrinth of Leadership

OVERSEER OF THE CHURCH

*"Be on guard for yourselves and for all the flock,
among which the Holy Spirit has made you overseers" (Acts 20:28).*

Although business measures the boss's success by "the bottom line," RobbinsNest thinks that "bodies, buildings, and bucks" (i.e., the ABCs of church growth: *a*ttendance, *b*uildings, and *c*ash) are the blessings, not benchmarks, of the pastor's office because he is an overseer of the church.

An overseer is a steward of kingdom resources, a watchman on the wall, a guardian of the faith. Though "administrivia" lifts its ugly head at times, pastors redeem the time with wisdom and clarity, not busyness and hurry. Calling, not activity, justifies their existence and their calendar.

****

As overseers, pastors watch over, care for, look after, uphold, and protect the C.H.U.R.C.H.'s . . .

Curriculum

- Who makes sure that orthodoxy and orthopraxy is taught to all age groups? *The pastor!*

    How do *you* see to this? _____

Hired staff

- Who keeps the staff *a*ccountable, *e*quipped, *i*nformed, ☺, and *u*nified? *The pastor!*

    How do *you* see to this? _____

Unity

- Who champions the kingdom reality of one body, though many members? *The pastor!*

    How do *you* see to this? _____

Resources

- Who insists that the church be a good steward of her facilities and finances? *The pastor!*

    How do *you* see to this? _____

Calendar

- Who cares that all of the events coincide with the purpose of the church? *The pastor!*

    How do *you* see to this? _____

History

- Who guards and defends the church's past, present, and future reputation? *The pastor!*

    How do *you* see to this? _____

Idea for the Overseer of the Church ⊃ Take a long prayer walk through the (1) church facility (e.g., pews, classrooms, offices, neighborhood, etc.), (2) church directory, and (3) church calendar.

Reflecting on the Labyrinth of Leadership

ROLE MODEL OF HOLINESS

"In all things show yourself to be an example of good deeds, with purity in doctrine, dignified, sound in speech which is beyond reproach" (Titus 2:7, 8).

Although a "holier than thou" attitude is to be avoided, RobbinsNest thinks pastors are to take seriously the commands "Come out from their midst and be separate" (2 Corinthians 6:17) and "Be perfect, as your heavenly Father is perfect" (Matthew 5:48) because they are role models of holiness.

> *What Do You Think?*
>
> Do you agree or disagree with the 19th-century pastor, Robert Murray M'Cheyne, when he stated, "My people's greatest need is my personal holiness"? If you agree, explain why. If you disagree, what would you say is your people's greatest need?

Following are some specific and unique opportunities for pastors to be role models of holiness:

- "In your going out and your coming in" (i.e., when you resign and candidate)
- In your private life (i.e., when nobody would know except for you and God)
- In your car after church (i.e., when your family hears what you really think)

FYI: "Those allotted to your charge" [and others] *are watching you*; thus "prove to be examples to the flock" [and to the others] (1 Peter 5:3). Preach the gospel, and, if necessary, use words.

****

Following are three applications available for the pastor. Yes, there is an **A.P.P.** for everything!

ACCOUNTABILITY

Do you have someone (e.g., a mentor, spiritual director, friend, et al.) to monitor and encourage "your progress and joy in the faith"? Who pays attention to God's heart regarding you, and to your heart regarding Him? Pastor, who pastors you?

PREPARATION

How could Jesus be "tempted in all things as we are, yet without sin" (Hebrews 4:15)? He was prepared! Although He was God, in His humanity Jesus trained for godliness (1 Timothy 4:7) through *transforming habits* ("As was His custom . . .").

PRAYER

Be the most prayed for and the most prayerful. Call on your retirees, shut-ins, and hospitalized to pray for you. They have time on their hands! And, yes, call on the Lord because He is the hero in your story. "There, but for the grace of God, go I."

****

Idea for the Role Model of Holiness ⊃ Find a quiet place to do the following "Release-Your-Body-to-God" spiritual exercise. In solitude and silence, lie down on the floor/ground (or sit down if need be) and surrender your body to God. Starting with your feet and making your way up to your head, ask God to take charge of each body part. Ask Him to fill it with His life and use it for His purposes. Accentuate the positive; do not just think of not sinning with your body.

Reflecting on the Labyrinth of Leadership

The following seven handouts reveal emphases on spiritual formation in eschatology—especially in Jesus' Olivet Discourse (Matthew 24-25). The acrostic of "P.r.e.a.c.h." will help guide you through this section of the labyrinth of leadership.

Use the space provided on the handouts and "Reflecting on the Labyrinth of Leadership" pages to answer questions and to record your thoughts during the spiritual exercises. Feel free to doodle, too.

*Take note that Jesus' entire "Olivet Discourse" (yes, all-of-it ☺) is included in the Appendix.

RobbinsNest Ministries
Stop. Look. Listen.

ESCHAMATION POINTS

Although "end times" is big business that feeds on narcissistic curiosity and misleads the masses, RobbinsNest thinks we are to practice what Jesus preached on end times (e.g., Olivet Discourse) because biblical eschatology serves, shapes, and schools our here and now spiritual formation.

Eschamation Points (emphases on formation in eschatology) cause paradigm shifts that shape not only our perspective and assessment of success, but also our progress and joy in the faith—both in this temporal arena and later in that eternal realm where we will rejoice and reign with God.

Eschamation Points steer us to wisely and correctly "learn Christ" (Ephesians 4:20). With this God-given second nature we progressively embody "Thy kingdom come" (i.e., eschatology) and "Thy will be done" (i.e., formation) as we travel along the boundary between time and eternity.

Eschamation Points provide the Church a larger historical perspective than visible objectives like fiscal years, building campaigns, and marketing blitzes. The fact that God is guiding history to a final goal provides endless more weight to the Christian community's significance and "brand."

Eschamation Points equip us to celebrate the image of God established in us *and* that at the core of existence is the Father, Son, and Holy Spirit, not protons, neutrons, and quarks. We join in the sweet society of the Godhead and bring to our churches and world the persons we are becoming.

"If you read history, you will find that the Christians who did most for the present world were precisely those who thought most of the next. . . . It is since Christians have largely ceased to think of the other world that they have become so ineffective in this. Aim at Heaven and you will get earth 'thrown in': aim at earth and you will get neither." (C.S. Lewis, *Mere Christianity*, 118)

Eschamation Points to P.r.e.a.c.h.

Following are six *Eschamation Points* (i.e., emphases on formation in eschatology) that Jesus makes in His Olivet Discourse. As we hear "all of it," it is clear that we are to practice what He did P.R.E.A.C.H.

PREPARATION ⊃ We ready ourselves for the long obedience.
REPENTANCE ⊃ We confess and turn from falling away, etc.
ENCOURAGEMENT ⊃ We see and help others to see that God is good.
ADORATION ⊃ We pick up a hymnbook, and not a crystal ball.
COMMUNITY ⊃ We journey together and we anticipate together.
HUMILITY ⊃ We see that history is Someone else's project.

Hear the Word of the Lord

Imagine yourself there on the Mount of Olives as you or someone else reads out loud Matthew 24–25. What *Eschamation Points*—emphases on spiritual formation in biblical eschatology—do you see?

Question: What has been your approach to eschatology? Have you fled from, ignored, or obsessed over it? Be honest with yourself and others.

Reflecting on the Labyrinth of Leadership

RobbinsNest Ministries
Stop. Look. Listen.

PREPARATION

"Behold, I have told you in advance" (24:25); "Therefore be on the alert" (24:42); "For this reason you also must be ready" (24:44); "The prudent took oil in flasks along with their lamps" (25:3)

Although the mindset of "we'll cross that bridge when it comes" and avoiding conflict is tempting, RobbinsNest thinks that *preparation* for the long obedience is one of Jesus' "Eschamation Points" because trials and tribulations are foreordained and inescapable until the final "Day of the Lord."

"End times" affects "now times." "Not yet" informs "already." Though the extended forecast calls for "scattered pain with a chance of martyrdom," we live and pastor along the edge of time and eternity with "righteousness, peace, and joy in the Holy Spirit" and in the light of Christ's return.

Preparation not only helps us to resist vices; it positions us to develop virtues. Like Jesus in His humanity, we can—by being prepared through spiritual disciplines—be tempted and yet not sin. As we "learn Christ" (Ephesians 4:20), we learn to purge any attraction to "missing the mark."

"As was His custom" (see Luke 4:16; 22:39, 41; Mark 10:1), Jesus engaged in such disciplines as:

_____

_____

With *preparation* as one of His Eschamation Points (i.e., emphases on formation in eschatology), Jesus wants to save us not only *from* the wails of regret; He wants to save us *for* the joy that comes with being the kinds of people who naturally do what He would do if He were in our shoes.

"Discipline yourself for the purpose of godliness" (1 Timothy 4:7) increasingly becomes the battle cry as end-times prophets and teachers deceive and anti-Christ rulers and terrorists persecute. The call is to train to reign and to take our place in God's ongoing creative work in His universe.

Eschamation Points to Reality

Those who have ears to hear and have hearts to welcome that God is guiding history to a final goal that He has revealed know where they are and where they are going.

Like with an upcoming sermon, driving test, or El Nino, *preparation* for the "Day of the Lord" is called for. "Be ready" is the wise course to take as the day draws near.

Contemplative Reading Exercise

Prayerfully read the parable of the ten virgins found in Matthew 25:1-13. Quietly reflect on Jesus' Eschamation Point of *preparation*; then discuss this point with others.

Eschamation Points to Dies Domini
"DAY OF THE LORD"

Throughout holy history God's people have been told about a coming "Day of the Lord"—a decisive divine intervention, a call to account, an unmistakable appearing, a victorious vindication, an unambiguous trouncing of evil, and a dispensing of divine blessings (including the restoration of Eden). See, for example, Joel 3:14; 2 Peter 3:10 ff.

Reflecting on the Labyrinth of Leadership

REPENTANCE

"At that time many will fall away and will betray one another and hate one another. Many false prophets will arise and will mislead many. Because lawlessness is increased, most people's love will grow cold" (24:10-12).

Although a growing number of Christian leaders act as if it is better to be right than to be good, RobbinsNest thinks that self-examination-driven *repentance* is one of Jesus' Eschamation Points because—in the end—"Well done, good and faithful servant" is not a grade on a doctrine exam.

"All Scripture [including the 33% of the Bible that is eschatological or apocalyptic] is inspired by God and profitable for teaching, for reproof, for correction, for training in righteousness; so that the man of God may be adequate, equipped for every good work" (2 Timothy 3:16-17).

What good is it to be pre-mill, post-mill, or a-mill if you fall away? What good is it to be pre-trib, mid-trib, or post-trib if your love grows cold? "End times" do not end times of examination. Thus, "Test yourselves to see if you are in the faith; examine yourselves!" (2 Corinthians 13:5).

Repentance includes turning from vices and turning to virtues. What should *you* turn from and to?

_____

_____

With *repentance* as one of His Eschamation Points (i.e., emphases on formation in eschatology), Jesus wants us to be aware of and beware of our and others' depravity. In times of impending change (be they pre-exilic or post-exilic), our call is to seek God and turn from our wicked ways.

"Surely not I, Lord?" (Matthew 26:22). Surely I will not betray You. I will not deny You. I will not doubt You. I will not . . . ↷ History proves that even the best of Jesus' disciples need *repentance*. "Therefore let him who thinks he stands take heed lest he fall" (1 Corinthians 10:12).

Eschamation Points to Persecution

The persecuted church exposes the American Church's complacency, presumptuousness, and half-heartedness. How ready are we for what (and who!) is coming soon?

While we want instant success (we have a wait problem!) and try to force the hand of God, our persecuted brothers and sisters wait upon the Lord to renew their strength.

Contemplative Reading Exercise

Prayerfully read Jesus' sermon introduction found in Matthew 24:1-14. Quietly reflect on His Eschamation Point of *repentance*; then discuss this point with others.

Eschamation Points to Imago Dei
"IMAGE OF GOD"

Though "God created man in His own image" (Genesis 1:27), that image has been cracked and defaced because of the fall; and thus is in need of being mended and made whole again. "But we all, with unveiled face beholding as in a mirror the glory of the Lord, are being transformed into the same image from glory to glory" (2 Corinthians 3:18).

Reflecting on the Labyrinth of Leadership

RobbinsNest Ministries
Stop. Look. Listen.

ENCOURAGEMENT

"For the sake of the elect those days will be cut short" (24:22); "Well done, good and faithful slave. You were faithful with a few things, I will put you in charge of many things; enter into the joy of your master" (25:21, 23)

Although the world around us increasingly inclines the majority to grow cynical and materialistic, RobbinsNest thinks *encouragement* (both received and given) is one of Jesus' Eschamation Points because life in God's kingdom is open to us now (and not just for the übermystical among us).

With *encouragement* as one of His Eschamation Points (i.e., emphases on formation in eschatology), Jesus wants us to see and show that present suffering doesn't compare to future splendor. He said, "In the world you have tribulation, but take courage; I have overcome the world" (John 16:33).

Encouragement forms us inside and out. Thus, be encouraged and be encouraging in "end times":

- Eschamation points to this: Our destiny includes being engaged in a tremendously creative team effort, with unimaginably splendid leadership, on an inconceivably vast plane of activity, with ever more comprehensive cycles of productivity and enjoyment.
- "We will not disappear into an eternal fog bank or dead storage, or exist in a state of isolation or suspended animation, as many seem to suppose. God has a much better use for us than that" (Dallas Willard, *The Divine Conspiracy*, 395). We will reign with Him!
- God has revealed that human life is a journey that ends neither in reincarnation nor in annihilation, but rather in resurrection! The divine Architect doesn't build a staircase that leads to nowhere. It leads to beauty, goodness, and into the sweet society of the Trinity.
- _____
- _____

Eschamation Points to Witnesses

"Since we have so great a cloud of witnesses surrounding us, let us also lay aside every encumbrance and the sin which so easily entangles us, and let us run with endurance the race that is set before us, fixing our eyes on Jesus, the author and perfecter of faith, who for the joy set before Him endured the cross, despising the shame, and has sat down at the right hand of the throne of God. For consider Him who has endured such hostility by sinners against Himself, so that you will not grow weary and lose heart."

Contemplative Reading Exercise

Prayerfully read the above text (Hebrews 12:1-3) and consider how it relates to the Eschamation Point of *encouragement*; then discuss your thoughts with others.

Eschamation Points to Visio Beatific
"BEATIFIC VISION"

"When He appears . . . we shall see Him just as He is" (1 John 3:2). We will have eyes fit to see from all angles that He is "holy, holy, holy." Until then, "We see in a mirror dimly, but then face to face" (1 Corinthians 13:12). Let us, therefore, be encouraged, for we can—by amazing grace on this side of eternity—train our "eyes" to see God with ever-increasing insight and discovery.

Reflecting on the Labyrinth of Leadership

ADORATION

"But when the Son of Man comes in His glory, and all the angels with Him, then He will sit on His glorious throne. All the nations will be gathered before Him . . ." (25:31, 32)

Although "end times" can feed curiosity (which is said to be the first step on the ladder of pride), RobbinsNest thinks *adoration*—not some figure-it-out-ism—is one of Jesus' Eschamation Points because a hymn book, not a crystal ball, takes us up and into God's grand story and our chief end.

With *adoration* as one of His Eschamation Points (i.e., emphases on formation in eschatology), Jesus expands our vision of who God is and what He calls us to be and to do on both sides of death. Because of this insight, we are better positioned to glorify God and enjoy Him forever.

The great hymns of the faith (especially in their last stanzas) often express "end times" *adoration*:

- [*All Hail the Power*] "O that with yonder sacred throng we at His feet may fall! We'll join the everlasting song, and crown Him Lord of all; we'll join the everlasting song, and crown Him Lord of all!"
- [*How Great Thou Art!*] "When Christ shall come with shout of acclamation and take me home, what joy shall fill my heart! Then I shall bow in humble adoration and there proclaim, my God, how great Thou art!"
- [*My Savior's Love*] "When with the ransomed in glory His face I at last shall see, 'twill be my joy thru the ages to sing of His love for me."
- [*The Solid Rock*] "When He shall come with trumpet sound, O may I then in Him be found, dressed in His righteousness alone, faultless to stand before the throne."

- [*Amazing Grace*] _____
- [   ] _____

Eschamation Points to Blessing

The Eschamation Point of *adoration* moves us to bless the Lord—to speak well about (*eulogia*) and give thanks for (*eucharistia*) the Most High God who is guiding history to a final goal that He Himself has already revealed.

The Berakah *Prayer of Blessing*

Ponder the remarkable realities of biblical eschatology. Then, beginning with the words "Blessed be the Lord who . . .", write out a *berakah* (a Hebrew form of prayer). Then, share it with others. Following is a *berakah* example:

- Blessed be the Lord who is worthy to unroll the scroll that contains the authorized and unabridged World Civilizations textbook (see Revelation 5).

> ### Eschamation Points to "GLORIA PATRI"
>
> *"Glory be to the Father, and to the Son, and to the Holy Ghost: as it was in the beginning, is now and ever shall be, world without end. Amen, amen."*
>
> May we sing with understanding (Colossians 3:16) this doxology that expresses to the Holy Trinity an ongoing "world-without-end" *adoration* that continues from this world to the next. So be it!

Reflecting on the Labyrinth of Leadership

 RobbinsNest Ministries
Stop. Look. Listen.

COMMUNITY

"The King will answer and say to them, 'Truly I say to you, to the extent that you did it to one of these brothers of Mine, even the least of them, you did it to Me'" (25:40).

Although "Everyone did what was right in his own eyes" (Judges 21:25) is applauded today, RobbinsNest thinks *community*—a life with and for others—is one of Jesus' Eschamation Points because, from the beginning in the garden to the end-times and beyond, life is not a private event.

With *community* as one of His Eschamation Points (i.e., emphases on formation in eschatology), Jesus affirms that we love God and neighbor together. There is no alternative. As Dallas Willard said, "The aim of God in history is the creation of an all-inclusive community of loving persons, with Himself included in that community as its prime sustainer and most glorious inhabitant."

Community is where everybody is somebody and Jesus Christ is Lord. "So then, while we have opportunity, let us do good to all people, and especially to those who are of the household of the faith" (Galatians 6:10). Contrasted to the climate of suspicion and loss of first-love in Ephesus (Revelation 2:4; cf. Ephesians 1:15) are the "one anothers" that embody *community*. For example:

"Serve one another" (Galatians 5:13); _____

_____

Note: At the Last Judgment the whole heavenly hosts and the whole human race (absolutely everybody from Adam and Eve on) will be assembled together in one place and time. This event will be the most significant mass meeting of all time—light years beyond a cosmic Woodstock! All who were given life will be present and accounted for at the consummation of world history.

Eschamation Points to Fellowship

The writer of Hebrews reminds us, "Let us consider how to stimulate one another to love and good deeds, not forsaking our own assembling together, as is the habit of some, but encouraging one another; and all the more as you see *the day drawing near*" (Hebrews 10:24-25).

And the Apostle Paul reminds us that we "proclaim the Lord's death *until He comes*" (1 Corinthians 11:26) when we gather together for the Lord's Supper (Communion).

Contemplative Reading Exercise

Prayerfully read the biblical texts cited on this one-page handout. Quietly reflect on the Eschamation Point of *community*; then discuss this point with others.

> ### *Eschamation Points to* Communio Sanctorum "COMMUNION OF SAINTS"
>
> The ultimate communion of saints is the Trinity. Pure *koinonia* abides within the Godhead. And the holy universal Church, made up of God's people on both sides of the grave, abides in and images forth this holy fellowship. United and dressed in Christ's righteousness, the saints cheer for one another as they run with endurance the race set before them (cf. Hebrews 12:1)—a race that has an approaching finish line.

Reflecting on the Labyrinth of Leadership

 RobbinsNest Ministries
Stop. Look. Listen.

HUMILITY

"But of that day and hour no one knows, not even the angels of heaven, nor the Son, but the Father alone" (24:36); "Therefore be on the alert, for you do not know which day your Lord is coming" (24:42)

Although being "in-the-know" and even forcing the hand of God can label a leader "ambitious," RobbinsNest thinks *humility* that abandons outcomes to God is one of Jesus' Eschamation Points because God—the One who is guiding history—is writing His story on the pages of our lives.

With *humility* as one of His Eschamation Points (i.e., emphases on formation in eschatology), Jesus prompts us to entrust results to God. Instead of shouldering the burden, we let God be God—for keeping a childlike sense of wonder, surprise, and need for guidance isn't beneath our dignity.

As our capacities decline and our responsibilities increase, we bump into reality—a reality that regularly reminds us of our inability to fulfill many of our earthly hopes and dreams. We pray for wisdom and strength as we grow in the knowledge that human history is Someone else's project.

Why are the "I-decoded-the-date" prophets and "newspaper eschatology" teachers so popular?

_____

_____

"It is not for you to know times or epochs which the Father has fixed by His own authority; but you will receive power when the Holy Spirit comes on you; and you shall be My witnesses both in Jerusalem, and in all Judea and Samaria, and even to the remotest part of the earth" (Acts 1:7, 8).

Humility releases us and rescues us from the grim captivity and ever-burdening weight of having to get our own way, get even, and get ahead. We welcome and embrace amazing grace—God acting in our lives to bring about what we do not deserve and cannot accomplish on our own.

Eschamation Points to Questions

Beginning (and continuing!) with *humility*, let us ponder matters regarding our practice of what Jesus did PREACH.

H ⮕ What if we actually did know "that day and hour"?
C ⮕ Is there a place for competition within the Church?
A ⮕ Why say, "He must increase, but I must decrease"?
E ⮕ Where do we look for hope during these end times?
R ⮕ How often should we pray, "Lord, have mercy"?
P ⮕ When do we come to Jesus . . . and learn from Him?

Contemplative Reading Exercise

Prayerfully read the biblical texts cited on this one-page handout. Quietly reflect on the Eschamation Point of *humility*; and then discuss this point with others.

Eschamation Points to Anno Domini
"IN THE YEAR OF THE LORD"

All of history is all about ~~me~~, ~~us~~, ~~you~~, Jesus Christ. Our Gregorian calendar is divided by His birth. Year 1 A.D. immediately follows year 1 B.C. ("Before Christ"). There is no year 0! Why? Because there is no time when Jesus was not. He was eternally preexistent before the incarnation and He is eternally existent after His birth. Whether past, present, or future, human history centers on Jesus.

Reflecting on the Labyrinth of Leadership

The following nine handouts focus on what Dallas Willard wants to say to pastors. His wisdom and insights (without an acrostic ☺) will help guide you through this section of the labyrinth of leadership.

Do write on the handouts as you encounter the various questions. Use the "Reflecting on the Labyrinth of Leadership" pages to take notes and record thoughts (and even doodle) as you engage in the various exercises.

*Note: An audio recording of "The Top Ten Things Dallas Willard Wants to Say to Pastors" is available at www.RobbinsNestMinistries.org.

KINGDOM PASTORS

Although the present state of the church leaves many leaders hopeless, RobbinsNest thinks these are extraordinary times to be kingdom pastors because, to echo Dallas Willard's prophetic voice, "We are on the verge of a time when the church is going to be able to make some decisions."

Dallas Willard spoke to the Board of Directors of RobbinsNest Ministries on October 10, 2010 (10/10/10) on the topic "The Top 10 Things Dallas Willard Wants to Say to Pastors." He shared 8!

1. Magnify your office
Although jokes about ministers are in vogue and many outside and inside the church belittle the position of pastor, RobbinsNest Ministries thinks it's time to magnify the office of pastor because they are called—as sent ambassadors—to "shepherd the flock of God among you" (1 Peter 5:2)!

2. Work in the power that is not your own or natural
Although pastors are hired with and evaluated by the expectation to take the church "to the next level," RobbinsNest thinks that business-driven results are unrealistic and counterproductive because God's kingdom pastors only work effectively in the power that is not their own or natural.

3. Work with the people who are there
Although many see outreach and worship as a marketing strategy, RobbinsNest thinks that pastors should evangelize the church and work with the people who are there because discipleship is the primary mission of the church (and is, in fact, what truly fuels worship and outreach).

4. Work out a biblical understanding of discipleship and make it the central focus of your life and ministry
Although common belief asserts that you can be a Christian without being a disciple, RobbinsNest thinks discipleship constitutes the Christian life because Jesus' call is to trust Him with your life, not just your death, and to learn from Him how to love God and neighbor in everyday life.

5. Preach and teach what Jesus did
Although doubt is considered virtuous and truth is seen as evolving in this post-modern world, RobbinsNest thinks that pastors are best positioned to preach and teach true and abiding knowledge about the availability and desirability of God's kingdom because that's what Jesus did.

6. Understand the pattern of spiritual growth
Although culture advocates mass-production and quick fixes, RobbinsNest thinks pastors should invest the time to expand peoples' vision of God, build their intention to be Jesus' disciples, and promote the means of grace because this forms the reliable pattern for spiritual formation.

7. Evaluate your practices in the church
Although days go by unexamined while day-planners fill up, RobbinsNest thinks pastors should create space and time to evaluate their practices in the church because this discipline positions and prepares them for new insights, clear intentions, and fresh means to lead as kingdom pastors.

8. Take care of yourself—rejoice in the Lord & don't carry the burden of success
Although statistics show that 50% of those who go into fulltime ministry will no longer be in ministry five years later, RobbinsNest thinks pastors can flourish and finish well because God routinely showers His amazing grace upon those who develop an enduring focus to their calling.

****

Question: What would you want to say to pastors? What would you add or subtract from the above?

Reflecting on the Labyrinth of Leadership

THE CALL

Although jokes about ministers are in vogue and many outside and inside the church belittle the position of pastor, RobbinsNest Ministries thinks it's time to magnify the office of pastor because they are called—as sent ambassadors—to "shepherd the flock of God among you" (1 Peter 5:2)!

The Apostle Paul understood that he was "*not sent from men nor through the agency of man, but through Jesus Christ and God the Father, who raised Him from the dead*" (Galatians 1:1). Paul—consistent with biblical revelation—thoroughly knew the God-centeredness of the calling.

- "*I will give you* shepherds after My own heart, who will feed you on knowledge and understanding" (Jeremiah 3:15).
- "*I will also raise up* shepherds over them and they will tend them" (Jeremiah 23:4).
- "*He [the triune God] gave* some as apostles, and some as prophets, and some as evangelists, and some as pastors and teachers, for the equipping of the saints[,] for the work of service, to the building up of the body of Christ" (Ephesians 4:11, 12).

We *receive* the call; we await God's beck and call. Pastors are *sent* ambassadors. They are not self-elevated. Otherwise, like with the false prophets of Jeremiah's day, God declares, "I did not send them or command them, nor do they furnish this people the slightest benefit" (Jeremiah 23:32).

The C.A.L.L. Checklist
(check appropriate boxes)

☐ CHARACTER AND CONDUCT. Do you possess the fruit of the Spirit (Galatians 5:23, 24) and the qualifications of a servant-leader (1 Timothy 3:2-7; Titus 1:6-9)? Have you cultivated holy habits and convictions? Do you recognize, understand, and obey God's voice?

☐ ABILITY AND FRUITFULNESS. Are you physically fit and spiritually gifted to pastor and teach? Is there evidence that God works through you to save sinners and to edify saints? Has the local church and those that know you best affirmed God's call on your life?

☐ LONGING AND AFFIRMATION. Do you have a deep, sustained desire to "shepherd the flock of God among you"? Have you entered your calling thoughtfully and intentionally, not perfunctorily or impulsively? Is there "fire in your bones"?

☐ LAYING ON OF HANDS. Have you been duly prepared (by schooling and life), examined (by an ordination committee), and authorized (by a local church) to carry out a representative ministry on behalf of the whole people (*laos*) of God?

Word of Warning

Many outside and inside the church belittle the position of pastor. Jokes about ministers are in vogue. Reverends are no longer revered. Patronizing flattery and veneered esteem are gestures (or else jesters) evoking the days when clergy were the most respected persons in the community.

Beyond not magnifying the office, there are those who target it. They aim to dislocate the call. "Strike the shepherd, and the sheep will be scattered" (Zechariah 13:7—NIV). "I know that after my departure savage wolves will come in among you, not sparing the flock" (Acts 20:29).

Reflecting on the Labyrinth of Leadership

WHAT DO YOU EXPECT?

Although pastors are hired with and evaluated by the expectation to take the church "to the next level," RobbinsNest thinks that business-driven results are unrealistic and counterproductive because God's kingdom pastors only work effectively in the power that is not their own or natural.

> [P]astoral work originates in and is shaped by the revelation of God in Jesus Christ. It takes place in the world's culture, but it is not caused by it. It is intimately involved in the world, but it is not defined by it. The gospel is free, not only in the sense that we don't have to pay for it, but also in the more fundamental sense that it is an expression of God's freedom—it is not caused by our needs but by God's grace. The Trinity—not the culture, not the congregation—is the primary context for acquiring training and understanding in the pastoral vocation.
> (Eugene Peterson, *The Unnecessary Pastor*, 5)

Unrealistic Expectations (derived from pleasing culture and congregants)

The Question: *Who sets the agenda?*

The Honest Answer: _____

Unfortunately, pastors assume they can do what they cannot do. They wear too many hats and have too many bosses. They are overwhelmed with "administrivia," "bigger is better," and "take it to the next level." And, they're put on a pedestal and live in a fishbowl.

Realistic Expectations (derived from knowing God and knowing yourself)

The Question: *Who works for whom?*

The Correct Answer: _____

God builds, gifts, and arms His church. He works for, in, and through His people—to His glory and their joy. Because He is omnipresent and omnipotent, a with-God life places confidence in the Holy Spirit, not the pride-filled flesh. We're free to entrust results to God.

****

- Have you saved a soul?   ○ Yes   ○ No   ○ Not Sure
- What "armor of God" do you especially need these days? _____

_____

- Are you a good pastor?   ○ Yes   ○ No   ○ Not Sure
- What "gifts of the Spirit" do you feel God has given you? _____

_____

Reflecting on the Labyrinth of Leadership

SIMPLY FI

Although many see outreach and worship as a marketing strategy, RobbinsNest thinks that pastors should evangelize the church and work with the people who are there because discipleship is the primary mission of the church (and is, in fact, what truly fuels worship and outreach).

Akin to the Marines' *Semper Fi* (Latin for "always faithful"), *Simply Fi* (Englatin ☺ for "simply faithful") is more than a motto to the pastorate; it is a way of life. Pastors simply stay faithful to their Commander, His people, and the mission at hand: "Work with the people who are there."

Simply Fi frees pastors to be faithful, not successful. Though never an excuse for idleness, this motto removes the burden of results. It simplifies their marching orders. They abandon outcomes to God, the One who truly does the work for us, in us, and through us—to His glory and our joy!

Faithful Witness

God's called and faithful pastors have much more than treasured traditions, personal opinions, or blind commitments. They have firsthand knowledge. They are witnesses and "missional" in the truest sense because they "speak that which [they] know, and bear witness of that which [they] have seen" (John 3:11). They witness by who they are—as do faithful parishioners. *Simply Fi!*

> We should note that witnesses are, first of all, those who *know* something. They don't just believe something. If you get on the 'witness stand' to tell people what you believe or feel strongly about, it will be of no use. That an individual believes something or has been told something is of little interest or importance. By contrast, the witness knows something and makes that knowledge available to others.
> (Dallas Willard, *Knowing Christ Today*, 195)

Inreach vs. Outreach

- Should we evangelize the church?   ○ Yes   ○ No   ○ Not Sure
- Should worship be a marketing strategy?   ○ Yes   ○ No   ○ Not Sure
- Does Matthew 28:19's "Go" mean "As you go"?   ○ Yes   ○ No   ○ Not Sure
- Is the primary instrument of evangelism the believer?   ○ Yes   ○ No   ○ Not Sure

****

○ True or ○ False: Pastors spend too much time thinking about those who are not in church.

○ True or ○ False: Pastors thank God for who is in church more than think about who is not.

Spiritual Exercise: Simply Pray

Spend some time praying for the people who are there . . .

- In your church
- In your family

Reflecting on the Labyrinth of Leadership

RobbinsNest Ministries
Stop. Look. Listen.

FOLLOWSHIP IN THE FELLOWSHIP

Although common belief asserts that you can be a Christian without being a disciple, RobbinsNest thinks discipleship constitutes the Christian life because Jesus' call is to trust Him with your life, not just your death, and to learn from Him how to love God and neighbor in everyday life.

Understanding Discipleship

Discipleship is apprenticeship. Jesus' disciples are students-for-life, learning to be with Him to be like Him. He said, "It is enough for the disciple that he become as his teacher" (Matthew 10:25).

Discipleship is being yoked to Jesus on the Way. Disciples learn from Him how to love God and neighbor in everyday life. He said, "Take My yoke upon you, and learn from Me" (Matthew 11:29).

Focusing upon Discipleship

Discipleship is to be the primary mission of the local church. Commissioned to "make disciples" (Matthew 28:19), we focus on one another's "progress and joy in the faith" (Philippians 1:25).

Discipleship authenticates and initiates evangelism in the local church. We share what we have (double the joy!). Jesus said, "Follow Me, and I will make you fishers of men" (Matthew 4:19).

What Do You Now Think?

❦ Can you be a Christian without being a disciple of Jesus?   ○ Yes   ○ No   ○ Not Sure

❦ Does discipleship in the local church cost a lot of money?   ○ Yes   ○ No   ○ Not Sure

○ True or ○ False: The cost of non-discipleship outweighs & outlasts the cost of discipleship.

○ True or ○ False: The definitions of "discipleship" and "spiritual formation" are identical.

⊃ Discipleship is _____
_____

Exercise: As you or someone else reads aloud the passage below (Matthew 19:16-22), imagine yourself overhearing the exchange between Jesus and the rich young man. What is your reaction?

One came to Jesus and said, "Teacher, what good thing shall I do that I may obtain eternal life?" He said to him, "Why are you asking Me about what is good? There is only One who is good; but if you wish to enter into life, keep the commandments. . . . The young man said to Him, "All these things I have kept; what am I still lacking?" Jesus said to him, "If you wish to be complete, go and sell your possessions and give to the poor, and you shall have treasure in heaven; and come, follow Me." But when the young man heard this statement, he went away grieved; for he was one who owned much property.

Reflecting on the Labyrinth of Leadership

RobbinsNest Ministries
Stop. Look. Listen.

WHAT'S IN YOUR MESSAGE?

Although doubt is considered virtuous and truth is seen as evolving in this post-modern world, RobbinsNest thinks that pastors are best positioned to preach and teach true and abiding knowledge about the availability and desirability of God's kingdom because that's what Jesus did.

From the very start, Jesus said, "*Repent, for the kingdom of heaven is at hand*" (Matthew 4:17).

- Jesus did *not* preach and teach:
  - "*Watch out*, for the doom of heaven is at hand."
  - "Repent, *in order for* the kingdom of heaven to come."
  - "Repent, for the kingdom of heaven is *just around the corner*."

- Jesus did preach and teach:
  - "*Repent*, for the kingdom of heaven is at hand."
    In effect, "Turn your attention toward God for your vision of Him is distorted. Change the way you think about Him. Stop thinking and feeling the way you do and start looking at reality the way I properly present it."
  - "Repent, for the *kingdom of heaven* is at hand."
    The kingdom of heaven is God acting (i.e., the range of His effective will).
  - "Repent, for the kingdom of heaven is *at hand*."
    Life with God is immediately available. The blessed "Welcome" sign is up!

> Advocates of modern religion rejected the concept of orthodoxy and believed that religious doctrines should be treated like scientific theories, constantly challenged and tested, revised and enlarged. "Orthodoxy is, in the Church, very much what prejudice is in a single mind. It is the premature conceit of certainty," observed Phillips Brooks, a leading liberal minister. Religious doctrine, like prejudice, must "be kept open for revision and enlargement, if it can be always aware of its partialness and imperfection, then it becomes simply a point of departure for newer worlds of thought and action, or we may say, a *working hypothesis* which is one stage of the progress toward truth." Change in religion, like change in science, was supposed to represent improvement and growth.
> (Julie A. Reuben, *The Making of the Modern University*, 97)

JESUS ANSWERED AND SAID TO [NICODEMUS], "TRULY, TRULY, I SAY TO YOU,
UNLESS ONE IS BORN AGAIN [I.E., BORN FROM ABOVE], HE CANNOT SEE THE KINGDOM OF GOD."
—JOHN 3:3—

True or False: Matthew 4:17 summarizes Jesus' total message.

True or False: God still uses preaching to establish His people.

True or False: Jesus expected us to develop His initial gospel.

****

Soteriology 101

Is salvation ➲ More about being saved *from* or *for* something?
　　　　　　 ➲ More about your life on earth or life in heaven?
　　　　　　 ➲ Being involved in what Jesus is doing on earth?

Reflecting on the Labyrinth of Leadership

RELIABLE PATTERN

Although culture advocates mass-production and quick fixes, RobbinsNest thinks pastors should invest the time to expand peoples' vision of God, build their intention to be Jesus' disciples, and promote the means of grace because this forms the reliable pattern for spiritual formation.

VISION: DO YOU HAVE A CLEAR AND VIVID UNDERSTANDING OF THE GOODNESS AND DESIRABILITY OF SPIRITUAL GROWTH?

INTENTION: HAVE YOU DECIDED AND MADE A SETTLED RESOLVE TO ADVANCE IN YOUR SPIRITUAL FORMATION?

MEANS: HAVE YOU INSTITUTED PARTICULAR ACTIVITIES AND ARRANGEMENTS THAT ARE SUITED TO CARRY YOUR INTENTION INTO THE REALITY OF YOUR VISION?

VISION: *Can you see . . .*

- Who God is and why He created you?
    - How big, beautiful, and good is your God? Did God create you because He was lonely?

- That you can have life with God now?
    - "Suppose that you were to die tonight and stand before God and He were to say to you, 'Why should I let you into My heaven?' What would you say?" Though a great diagnostic question, it does make you wonder: What if I do not die tonight? Is there a gospel for me?

INTENTION: *Do you aim and plan to . . .*

- Do God's will completely, cheerfully, and without hesitation?
    - How is God's will done in heaven? (". . . Thy will be done, on earth as it is in heaven . . .")

- Have an ongoing, interactive, ever-deepening relationship with God?
    - Are you a disciple of Jesus, one who abides in His presence and takes on His character?

MEANS: *As you journey on the road of transformation, ask yourself . . .*

- How would Jesus live my life if He were me?
    - What thoughts, attitudes, and actions would He have if He were in your shoes?

- How was Jesus tempted like you are, and yet not sin?
    - Answer: He was prepared.

The phrase "*as was His custom*" is used three times by the Gospel writers when referring to Jesus (Luke 4:16; Luke 22:39; Mark 10:1). These references inform us as to some of the transforming habits Jesus engaged in on a regular basis (for example, worship, fellowship, solitude, study, & prayer).

Has this pattern of spiritual formation been reliable for you?

Reflecting on the Labyrinth of Leadership

H.O.N.E.S.T. EVALUATION

Although most organizations focus on and stress over the outcomes and results of their events, RobbinsNest thinks there is a better and more HONEST way to approach events when evaluating because God calls us to be faithful and to entrust the results and abandon the outcomes to Him.

> *As we evaluate this particular event, let us ask, "Were we honest in our . . .*
>
> **HUMILITY** ⊃ Were we respectful, kind, and attentive to all the participants?
> **OBEDIENCE** ⊃ Were we faithful to following God's direction and schedule?
> **NOTIFICATIONS** ⊃ Were we truthful in promotional advertising and offers?
> **EFFORTS** ⊃ Were we diligent in pre-event prayer, planning, and preparation?
> **STEWARDSHIP** ⊃ Were we above board with assets and money (to the penny)?
> **TOPIC** ⊃ Was the subject matter biblical and consistent with our mission?

HUMILITY   ○ YES   ○ MOSTLY   ○ MOSTLY NOT   ○ NO   ⊃ HERE'S WHY & HOW:
Did we honestly (a) see people as ends, not means to our ends?   ▪ _____
(b) "work the room" with real servants' hearts?   ▪ _____

OBEDIENCE   ○ YES   ○ MOSTLY   ○ MOSTLY NOT   ○ NO   ⊃ HERE'S WHY & HOW:
Did we honestly (a) have God's will, not sacred cows, to guide us?   ▪ _____
(b) "stop, look, listen" and then make decisions?   ▪ _____

NOTIFICATIONS   ○ YES   ○ MOSTLY   ○ MOSTLY NOT   ○ NO   ⊃ HERE'S WHY & HOW:
Did we honestly (a) do what we said we'd do (no bait & switch)?   ▪ _____
(b) report on the event (not inflate numbers, etc.)?   ▪ _____

EFFORTS   ○ YES   ○ MOSTLY   ○ MOSTLY NOT   ○ NO   ⊃ HERE'S WHY & HOW:
Did we honestly (a) ask & plan for God to "show up & show off"?   ▪ _____
(b) follow through on being organized and ready?   ▪ _____

STEWARDSHIP   ○ YES   ○ MOSTLY   ○ MOSTLY NOT   ○ NO   ⊃ HERE'S WHY & HOW:
Did we honestly (a) use money and love people, not vice versa?   ▪ _____
(b) handle the money as it came in and went out?   ▪ _____

TOPIC   ○ YES   ○ MOSTLY   ○ MOSTLY NOT   ○ NO   ⊃ HERE'S WHY & HOW:
Did we honestly (a) use the Bible (not rubber Bible) for the theme?   ▪ _____
(b) reflect the ministry's mission in the material?   ▪ _____

Reflecting on the Labyrinth of Leadership

CARE TO FOCUS & FOCUS TO CARE

Although statistics show that 50% of those who go into fulltime ministry will no longer be in ministry five years later, RobbinsNest thinks pastors can flourish and finish well because God routinely showers His amazing grace upon those who develop an enduring focus to their calling.

> The Apostle Paul was able to say in the end,
> *"I have fought the good fight, I have finished the course, I have kept the faith."*
> (2 Timothy 4:7)

What constitutes flourishing and finishing well? This question is of utmost importance for you, pastor, to answer if you are to "take care of yourself—rejoice in the Lord and not carry the burden of success." Bathed in God's grace, flourishing and finishing well involves an enduring . . .

- **Faithfulness to God's calling**—in the midst of life's persistent questions and trials, "We do not lose heart" (2 Corinthians 4:16).
- **Obedience to God's will**—there is a continuing growth in godliness (i.e., love for God and neighbor in everyday life; cf. Hebrews 13:7).
- **Commitment to learning**—research and development (i.e., reading, schooling, seminars, conferences, mentors, etc.) is a part of life.
- **Unity of purpose**—the whole person (spiritually, physically, emotionally, relationally, etc.) is set on glorifying God and enjoying Him forever.
- **Sanctification of success**—the important thing is not what we accomplish but the person we become (i.e., our character, not our credentials).

Pastor, you can flourish and finish well. Look at Jesus, *the* Pastor of pastors. He had an enduring focus and lived with the end in mind; and He above all others flourished and finished well! He is the One to rejoice in and to abandon outcomes to because He is "the author and finisher of faith."

Focus on F.O.C.U.S. for Focus

Which point(s) particularly prepares and positions *you* to "take care of yourself . . ."?	Which point(s) have *you* compromised on or abandoned in the pastorate?	What point(s) would *you* add to F.O.C.U.S.? (e.g., beware of addictions and distractions)

****

"For the herald of the gospel to be spiritually out of order in his own proper person is, both to himself and to his work, a most serious calamity; and yet, my brethren, how easily is such an evil produced, and with what watchfulness must it be guarded against!" (Charles Haddon Spurgeon)

Reflecting on the Labyrinth of Leadership

The following five handouts focus on odds and ends for "Transforming Pastors." These stand-alone topics will help guide you through this last-but-not-least section of the labyrinth of leadership.

Write on the handouts and "Reflecting on the Labyrinth of Leadership" pages as you encounter questions to ponder and spiritual exercises to engage in. Take notes, as well as record your experiences, ideas, and insights—and doodle.

*Take note that all 52 "Although... RobbinsNest thinks... Because..." theses are included in the Appendix.

RobbinsNest Ministries
Stop. Look. Listen.

ADVENTUALITY

"The Sunrise from on high shall visit us, to shine upon those who sit in darkness and the shadow of death, to guide our feet into the way of peace" (Luke 1:78-79).

Although pop-Christianity sees spirituality as a wave to ride now or an option to consider later, RobbinsNest thinks the coming of spirituality in Jesus—*adventuality*—is at hand and to be hailed because being with Jesus to become like Jesus is *"the* Way," not a passing wave, of Christianity.

Adventuality is more than an eventuality. Learning to live as God intends through an interactive relationship with the living Lord isn't a mere likelihood that can happen for disciples; the advent of Christ-like spirituality has commenced and will continue to advance throughout all eternity.

Adventuality ⊃ "For the grace of God has appeared [i.e., Jesus' first advent], bringing salvation to all men, instructing us to deny ungodliness and worldly desires and to live sensibly, righteously and godly in the present age [i.e., Christ-like spirituality], looking for the blessed hope and the appearing of the glory of our great God and Savior, Christ Jesus [i.e., Jesus' second advent], who gave Himself for us to redeem us from every lawless deed, and to purify for Himself a people for His own possession, zealous for good deeds [i.e., Christ-like spirituality]" (Titus 2:11-14).

Adventuality—the coming of spirituality in Jesus—brings us hope that we will bear the fruit of the Spirit between the first and second comings of Christ and beyond. The "love, joy, peace, . . ." of God, from God, and with God will be evident and experienced as we live out the with-God life.

List some practical ways *you* can thank God for His past grace and trust God for His future grace:

_____

_____

Questions to Ponder and Discuss

T or F - We will instantly become perfect when we die.

T or F - We take our memories and character to heaven.

T or F - We train now on earth to reign later in heaven.

T or F - We finally give to God the people we become.

Contemplative Reading Exercise

Prayerfully read Luke 1:78-79 cited at the top of this one-page handout. Quietly reflect on the need for, and the effects of, *Adventuality*; then discuss your thoughts and insights on the coming of spirituality in Jesus with others.

*For further reflection, wake up tomorrow morning for the sunrise. "Stop, look, listen" as the Sunrise visits *you*!

In the **CHRISTIAN CALENDAR**, the season of *Advent* prepares us to:

- Celebrate the first coming of Jesus Christ (His blessed birth)
&
- Anticipate the second coming of Jesus Christ (our blessed hope).

During Advent, we focus on the

- Hope
- Peace
- Joy
- Love

that we have in His two comings.

Reflecting on the Labyrinth of Leadership

 RobbinsNest Ministries
Stop. Look. Listen.

SPIRITUAL FORMATION

> Long my imprisoned spirit lay
> Fast bound in sin and nature's night.
> Thine eye diffused a quick'ning ray:
> I woke—the dungeon flamed with light!
> My chains fell off, my heart was free,
> I rose, went forth, and followed Thee.
> (Charles Wesley, *And Can It Be?*)

Although the bifurcation of justification and sanctification minimizes the latter in some theological camps, RobbinsNest thinks spiritual formation is central to salvation because your "progress and joy in the faith" (Philippians 1:25) continues "until Christ is formed in you" (Galatians 4:19).

Christian spiritual formation is the process by which we become, by the Spirit's leading, the kind of people who routinely and naturally take on the character of Christ. It's the journey on the Way, the learning to obey all that Christ commanded us (Matthew 28:20), the bearing of the fruit of the Spirit (Galatians 5:22, 23), the "I rose, went forth, and followed Thee" part of the *ordo salutis*.

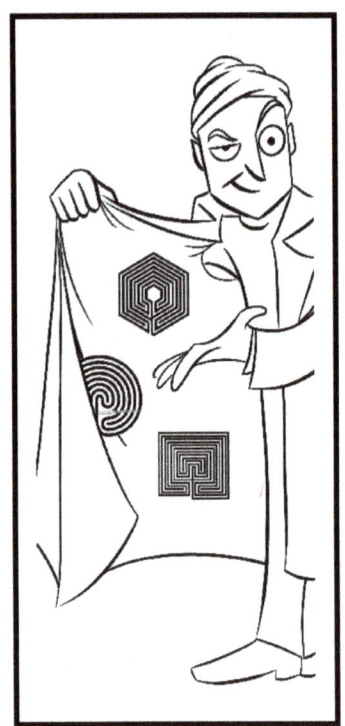

ORDO SALUTIS

For Calvinism:
1. Election (predestination & foreknowledge)
2. Effectual call (gospel call & inner call)
3. Regeneration (new birth & re-creation)
4. Conversion (faith & repentance)
5. Justification (declared righteous & forgiven)
6. Sanctification (growth & perseverance)
7. Glorification (resurrection & eternal life)

For Arminianism:
1. Outward call
2. Faith
3. Repentance
4. Regeneration
5. Justification
6. Perseverance
7. Glorification

Calvinists see faith as an effect *of election. Arminians see it as a* cause.

✳✳✳✳✳✳✳✳✳✳✳✳

Some in the Christian community perceive the current spiritual formation movement to be a **S.C.A.M.** They see it (*Do you?*) to be:

Syncretistic (It's "Christianity And"... New Age, Gnosticism, etc.)
Catholic (It's steeped in monasticism and/or works-righteousness.)
Argument from Silence (It's not explicitly mentioned in the Bible.)
Mystical (It's a form of Christian elitism, bordering on the occult.)

Naming Our Core Values

- Would you consider "Spiritual Formation" a core value? ○ Yes ○ No ○ I am not sure
- If "Yes," then how does one see this core value demonstrated in your life and ministry?

Spiritual Formation Idea ⊃ After you do your sermon-prep exegesis, meditate upon the pericopy.

Reflecting on the Labyrinth of Leadership

Writing a "Rule" for Life

Although crowds of time-wasters and hedon-chasers contend with their wayward, unruly lives, RobbinsNest thinks pastors and churches work best with a "rule" for life in place and in process because God designed us to live out our numbered days here on earth with wisdom and strength.

If you fail to plan, then you plan to fail. This modern proverb, like most proverbs, was formed by many failures observed, encountered, and repeated over time. Wisdom points to the fact that we need to be intentional. We need to have a plan, a strategy, a rhythm, a RULE FOR LIFE on the Way.

The most famous rule for monastic life is *The Rule of Saint Benedict*. But what about a rule for twenty-first-century pastoral life? What defines and details a pastor's intentions? How does he want to live? What is on his "To Be" and "To Do" lists—realistic expectations to be pursued?

Time is at hand to state your *Vision-Intention-Means* for the kind of life that you desire to live. As you prepare to write and record your "R.U.L.E." for life, take note that it should be . . .

- *Realistic*
  The rule should be applicable and practical, useful and appropriate for the real world.

- *Unified*
  The rule should be cohesive and balanced, bringing together the various dimensions of life.

- *Lived*
  The rule should be put into practice, indeed taking place and happening in everyday life.

- *Evaluated*
  The rule should be S.M.A.R.T.: Specific, Measurable, Attainable, Realistic, and Time-based.

Note: You can choose to write your "Rule" on your own, or you can choose to collaborate with others (e.g., make it a collective exercise with your church staff, elders, or small group).

Samples & Examples

As a pastor, I will . . .

- *Be still*. I will set aside two hours weekly and two whole days annually for solitude/silence.
- *Be on time*. I will arrive at least five minutes early to scheduled meetings and appointments.
- *Be a blessing*. I will do a home blessing monthly and publically praise a parishioner weekly.

As a church, we will . . .

- *Remember the Lord's Day*. We will prioritize the Sunday morning service by arriving early.
- *Remember the Lord's Supper*. We will prepare beforehand for this rite with self-examination.
- *Remember the Lord's Prayer*. We will pray this prayer each week at church for one year.

Spiritual Exercise: Begin to write *your* RULE FOR LIFE. What would be Rule #1 on your list?

Reflecting on the Labyrinth of Leadership

So What's Leadership?

Although publishers saturate the market with the latest experts' must-have leadership ideologies, RobbinsNest thinks budding and veteran leaders need only to look to Jesus' teaching and example because He has the best information on the most important topics, including what's a leader to do.

Question: What is the key to effective leadership in the church?
Answer: An ongoing, interactive, ever-deepening relationship with Jesus.

Period. There is no comma, semi-colon, colon, or em dash after Jesus. "Leaders" have Him lead. He forms their character and conduct. They welcome Him to work for, in, and through them—to His glory and their joy. They cooperate with Him as He writes His-story on the pages of their lives.

So what's a "leader" to do?

"Leaders" expand their *vision* of who Jesus is and what He calls them to be and do. To eliminate distractions and compromises—man-centered and market-driven principles—they focus their attention on Jesus. They are His students for life; learning from Him how to live, love, and serve.

Question: Do "leaders" need a program or product to be effective?
Answer: No. "Leaders" need a path upon which to proceed to follow Jesus.

"Leaders" hear and obey "Follow Me," not "Follow this." They follow divine footprints, not human blueprints, as they proceed to do kingdom business. They encounter and embrace "followership," not "administrivia," on the narrow road. They are pilgrims, not programmers.

So what's a "leader" to do?

"Leaders" build up their *intention* to be disciples of Jesus. To remove the burden of having to make things happen—meet or surpass projected goals and "guaranteed" results—they learn from Jesus how to abandon outcomes to God and how to not be pushy, prideful, and presumptuous.

Question: How do we develop and maintain such a relationship?
Answer: By creating space and making time to "stop, look, listen" to Jesus.

Following His lead, "leaders" prepare themselves for service through spiritual discipline. They do not assume character or excuse conduct. Instead of getting fed up, used up, or finally giving up, they engage in transforming habits, thus positioning themselves for God's kingdom service.

So what's a "leader" to do?

"Leaders" engage in *means* of transforming habits. To relax the grip of the two infamous gripes—"we've never done it like that before" and "we've always done it that way"—they pay attention to Jesus through such spiritual disciplines as solitude, contemplative study, and prayer.

Leadership is _____

_____

Reflecting on the Labyrinth of Leadership

PASTORINTH

Although the expected and celebrated pace of modern ministry remains conducive to a racetrack, RobbinsNest thinks pastors must slow down and relentlessly eliminate hurry from their lives because the pace of grace creates space and time for God to act in the labyrinth of leadership.

For centuries Christians have used labyrinths for their prayer walks. The one-course-with-many-curves (unicursal) path leading to a center place presents a metaphor of a spiritual pilgrimage to one's core and then back to one's community—hopefully with renewed focus and clarity. A labyrinth is a path to walk in, not a maze to figure out. It places before you a journey to savor, not a puzzle to solve. Unlike a maze that has a series of dead ends, for a labyrinth, the only way in is the only way out. The former requires logic and luck. The latter presents space and grace.

For the pastor, the journey inward involves examination of self and church. Movement to the center—a treasured rest in and awareness of our chief end—requires the removal of the masks and barriers we use to hide our true self. It's time to be honest and transparent—reality! Movement outward, then, becomes a time of new insights, clear intentions, and fresh means.

Walking this "pastorinth" on the Way releases us to venture onward with an appreciation for past grace and a trust for future grace. The process creates space and time to evaluate our traditions and practices. Why do we do the things we do? What do we need to change or not change? Nevertheless, we do not exit the pastorinth announcing a new revolution (e.g., "We're now all going to be disciples." "We are a church-planting church." Etc.) Because change can be upsetting, pastors wisely begin with teaching and preaching, and then bring in processes that will prepare the people for the change.

Prayer W.A.L.K. Exercise (Note: You can do this prayer walk on a labyrinth, or not. Your choice.)

1. *Wait on the Lord*. Take a few deep breaths. Quiet your spirit and center your thoughts on God. Begin your prayer walk with holy expectation.
2. *Attend to kingdom matters*. As you walk, address issues that God and you view as important. Be open to examine your character and church.

    Note: Your mind may wander as you walk. As Thomas à Kempis confessed in *The Imitation of Christ*, "While my mind thinks of heavenly things, a disorderly mob of carnal thoughts confronts my prayers." If and when this happens, do not fret. Simply return to business.
3. *Listen to the Lord*. What does He wish to say to you? Allow His Spirit to talk with your spirit. Be attentive to God-given insights and direction.
4. *Keep up the good work*. Maintain an attitude of prayer and attention to God throughout the day. Be aware: God works outside the pastorinth, too.

Reflecting on the Labyrinth of Leadership

Appendix

- Watch for Transforming Habits
- Scaffold for Building Leaders (John 13-17)
- Write Your Own Eulogy
- "I Magnify My Office" (Litany of Affirmation)
- Olivet Discourse (Matthew 24-25)
- The Fifty-Two "Although . . . RobbinsNest Thinks . . . Because . . ." Thesis Statements

- Works Cited
- RobbinsNest Ministries
- Books by Stephen W. Robbins

SCAFFOLD FOR BUILDING LEADERS
JOHN 13–17

1A SERVICE TO OTHERS (13:1-20)

[*Chapter 13*] (1) Now before the Feast of the Passover, Jesus knowing that His hour had come that He would depart out of this world to the Father, having loved His own who were in the world, He loved them to the end. (2) During supper, the devil having already put into the heart of Judas Iscariot, the son of Simon, to betray Him, (3) Jesus, knowing that the Father had given all things into His hands, and that He had come forth from God and was going back to God, (4) got up from supper, and laid aside His garments; and taking a towel, He girded Himself. (5) Then He poured water into the basin, and began to wash the disciples' feet and to wipe them with the towel with which He was girded. (6) So He came to Simon Peter. He said to Him, "Lord, do You wash my feet?" (7) Jesus answered and said to him, "What I do you do not realize now, but you will understand hereafter." (8) Peter said to Him, "Never shall You wash my feet!" Jesus answered him, "If I do not wash you, you have no part with Me." (9) Simon Peter said to Him, "Lord, then wash not only my feet, but also my hands and my head." (10) Jesus said to him, "He who has bathed needs only to wash his feet, but is completely clean; and you are clean, but not all of you." (11) For He knew the one who was betraying Him; for this reason He said, "Not all of you are clean." (12) So when He had washed their feet, and taken His garments and reclined at the table again, He said to them, "Do you know what I have done to you? (13) You call Me Teacher and Lord; and you are right, for so I am. (14) If I then, the Lord and the Teacher, washed your feet, you also ought to wash one another's feet. (15) For I gave you an example that you also should do as I did to you. (16) Truly, truly, I say to you, a slave is not greater than his master, nor is one who is sent greater than the one who sent him. (17) If you know these things, you are blessed if you do them. (18) I do not speak of all of you. I know the ones I have chosen; but it is that the Scripture may be fulfilled, 'He who eats My bread has lifted up his heel against Me.' (19) From now on I am telling you before it comes to pass, so that when it does occur, you may believe that I am He. (20) Truly, truly, I say to you, he who receives whomever I send receives Me; and he who receives Me receives Him who sent Me."

2A CONFRONT WITH CARE (13:21–14:15)

(21) When Jesus had said this, He became troubled in spirit, and testified and said, "Truly, truly, I say to you, that one of you will betray Me." (22) The disciples began looking at one another, at a loss to know of which one He was speaking. (23) There was reclining on Jesus' bosom one of His disciples, whom Jesus loved. (24) So Simon Peter gestured to him, and said to him, "Tell us who it is of whom He is speaking." (25) He, leaning back thus on Jesus' bosom, said to Him, "Lord, who is it?" (26) Jesus then answered, "That is the one for whom I shall dip the morsel and give it to him." So when He had dipped the morsel, He took and gave it to Judas, the son of Simon Iscariot. (27) After the morsel, Satan then entered into him. Therefore Jesus said to him, "What you do, do quickly." (28) Now no one of those reclining at the table knew for what purpose He had said this to him. (29) For some were supposing, because Judas had the money box, that Jesus was saying to him, "Buy the things we have need of for the feast"; or else, that he should give something to the poor. (30) So after receiving the morsel he went out immediately; and it was night. (31) Therefore when he had gone out, Jesus said, "Now is the Son of Man glorified, and God is glorified in Him; (32) if God is glorified in Him, God will also glorify Him in Himself, and will glorify Him immediately. (33) Little children, I am with you a little while longer. You will seek Me; and as I said to the Jews, now I also say to you, 'Where I am going, you cannot come.' (34) A new commandment I give to you, that you love one another, even as I have loved you, that you also love one another. (35) By this all men will know that you are My disciples, if you have love for one another." (36) Simon Peter said to Him, "Lord, where are You going?" Jesus answered, "Where I go, you cannot follow Me now; but you will follow later." (37) Peter said to Him, "Lord, why can I not follow You right now? I will lay down my life for You." (38) Jesus answered, "Will you lay down your life for Me? Truly, truly, I say to you, a rooster will not crow until you deny Me three times. [*Chapter 14*] (1) Do not let your heart be troubled; believe in God, believe also in Me. (2) In My Father's house are many dwelling places; if it were not so, I would have told you; for I go to prepare a place for you. (3) If I go and prepare a place for you, I will come again and receive you to Myself, that where I am, there you may be also. (4) And you know the way where I am going." (5) Thomas said to Him, "Lord, we do not know where You are going, how do we know the way?" (6) Jesus said to him, "I am the way, and the truth, and the life; no one comes to the Father but through Me. (7) If you had known Me, you would have known My Father also; from now on you know Him, and have seen Him." (8)

Philip said to Him, "Lord, show us the Father, and it is enough for us." (9) Jesus said to him, "Have I been so long with you, and yet you have not come to know Me, Philip? He who has seen Me has seen the Father; how can you say, 'Show us the Father'? (10) Do you not believe that I am in the Father, and the Father is in Me? The words that I say to you I do not speak on My own initiative, but the Father abiding in Me does His works. (11) Believe Me that I am in the Father and the Father is in Me; otherwise believe because of the works themselves. (12) Truly, truly, I say to you, he who believes in Me, the works that I do, he will do also; and greater works than these he will do; because I go to the Father. (13) Whatever you ask in My name, that will I do, so that the Father may be glorified in the Son. (14) If you ask Me anything in My name, I will do it. (15) If you love Me, you will keep My commandments."

3A Abide in Christ (14:16–15:11)

(16) "I will ask the Father, and He will give you another Helper, that He may be with you forever; (17) that is the Spirit of truth, whom the world cannot receive, because it does not see Him or know Him, but you know Him because He abides with you and will be in you. (18) I will not leave you as orphans; I will come to you. (19) After a little while the world will no longer see Me, but you will see Me; because I live, you will live also. (20) In that day you will know that I am in My Father, and you in Me, and I in you. (21) He who has My commandments and keeps them is the one who loves Me; and he who loves Me will be loved by My Father, and I will love him and will disclose Myself to him." (22) Judas (not Iscariot) said to Him, "Lord, what then has happened that You are going to disclose Yourself to us and not to the world?" (23) Jesus answered and said to him, "If anyone loves Me, he will keep My word; and My Father will love him, and We will come to him and make Our abode with him. (24) He who does not love Me does not keep My words; and the word which you hear is not Mine, but the Father's who sent Me. (25) These things I have spoken to you while abiding with you. (26) But the Helper, the Holy Spirit, whom the Father will send in My name, He will teach you all things, and bring to your remembrance all that I said to you. (27) Peace I leave with you; My peace I give to you; not as the world gives do I give to you. Do not let your heart be troubled, nor let it be fearful. (28) You heard that I said to you, 'I go away, and I will come to you.' If you loved Me, you would have rejoiced because I go to the Father, for the Father is greater than I. (29) Now I have told you before it happens, so that when it happens, you may believe. (30) I will not speak much more

with you, for the ruler of the world is coming, and he has nothing in Me; (31) but so that the world may know that I love the Father, I do exactly as the Father commanded Me. Get up, let us go from here." [*Chapter 15*] (1) "I am the true vine, and My Father is the vinedresser. (2) Every branch in Me that does not bear fruit, He takes away; and every branch that bears fruit, He prunes it so that it may bear more fruit. (3) You are already clean because of the word which I have spoken to you. (4) Abide in Me, and I in you. As the branch cannot bear fruit of itself unless it abides in the vine, so neither can you unless you abide in Me. (5) I am the vine, you are the branches; he who abides in Me and I in him, he bears much fruit, for apart from Me you can do nothing. (6) If anyone does not abide in Me, he is thrown away as a branch and dries up; and they gather them, and cast them into the fire and they are burned. (7) If you abide in Me, and My words abide in you, ask whatever you wish, and it will be done for you. (8) My Father is glorified by this, that you bear much fruit, and so prove to be My disciples. (9) Just as the Father has loved Me, I have also loved you; abide in My love. (10) If you keep My commandments, you will abide in My love; just as I have kept My Father's commandments and abide in His love. (11) These things I have spoken to you so that My joy may be in you, and that your joy may be made full."

FRUIT-BEARING FRIEND OF JESUS (15:12-17)

(12) "This is My commandment, that you love one another, just as I have loved you. (13) Greater love has no one than this, that one lay down his life for his friends. (14) You are My friends if you do what I command you. (15) No longer do I call you slaves, for the slave does not know what his master is doing; but I have called you friends, for all things that I have heard from My Father I have made known to you. (16) You did not choose Me but I chose you, and appointed you that you would go and bear fruit, and that your fruit would remain, so that whatever you ask of the Father in My name He may give to you. (17) This I command you, that you love one another."

3B OUTCAST IN WORLD (15:18–16:11)

(18) "If the world hates you, you know that it has hated Me before it hated you. (19) If you were of the world, the world would love its own; but because you are not of the world, but I chose you

out of the world, because of this the world hates you. (20) Remember the word that I said to you, 'A slave is not greater than his master.' If they persecuted Me, they will also persecute you; if they kept My word, they will keep yours also. (21) But all these things they will do to you for My name's sake, because they do not know the One who sent Me. (22) If I had not come and spoken to them, they would not have sin, but now they have no excuse for their sin. (23) He who hates Me hates My Father also. (24) If I had not done among them the works which no one else did, they would not have sin; but now they have both seen and hated Me and My Father as well. (25) But they have done this to fulfill the word that is written in their Law, 'They hated Me without a cause.' (26) When the Helper comes, whom I will send to you from the Father, that is the Spirit of truth who proceeds from the Father, He will testify about Me, (27) and you will testify also, because you have been with Me from the beginning. [*Chapter 16*] (1) These things I have spoken to you so that you may be kept from stumbling. (2) They will make you outcasts from the synagogue, but an hour is coming for everyone who kills you to think that he is offering service to God. (3) These things they will do because they have not known the Father or Me. (4) But these things I have spoken to you, so that when their hour comes, you may remember that I told you of them. These things I did not say to you at the beginning, because I was with you. (5) But now I am going to Him who sent Me; and none of you asks Me, 'Where are You going?' (6) But because I have said these things to you, sorrow has filled your heart. (7) But I tell you the truth, it is to your advantage that I go away; for if I do not go away, the Helper will not come to you; but if I go, I will send Him to you. (8) And He, when He comes, will convict the world concerning sin and righteousness and judgment; (9) concerning sin, because they do not believe in Me; (10) and concerning righteousness, because I go to the Father and you no longer see Me; (11) and concerning judgment, because the ruler of this world has been judged."

2B LISTEN WITH CARE (16:12-33)

(12) "I have many more things to say to you, but you cannot bear them now. (13) But when He, the Spirit of truth, comes, He will guide you into all the truth; for He will not speak on His own initiative, but whatever He hears, He will speak; and He will disclose to you what is to come. (14) He will glorify Me, for He will take of Mine and will disclose it to you. (15) All things that the Father has are Mine; therefore I said that He takes of Mine and will disclose it to you. (16) A little while, and you will no longer see Me; and again a little while, and you will see Me." (17)

Some of His disciples then said to one another, "What is this thing He is telling us, 'A little while, and you will not see Me; and again a little while, and you will see Me'; and, 'because I go to the Father'? (18) So they were saying, "What is this that He says, 'A little while'? We do not know what He is talking about." (19) Jesus knew that they wished to question Him, and He said to them, "Are you deliberating together about this, that I said, 'A little while, and you will not see Me, and again a little while, and you will see Me'? (20) Truly, truly, I say to you, that you will weep and lament, but the world will rejoice; you will grieve, but your grief will be turned into joy. (21) Whenever a woman is in labor she has pain, because her hour has come; but when she gives birth to the child, she no longer remembers the anguish because of the joy that a child has been born into the world. (22) Therefore you too have grief now; but I will see you again, and your heart will rejoice, and no one will take your joy away from you. (23) In that day you will not question Me about anything. Truly, truly, I say to you, if you ask the Father for anything in My name, He will give it to you. (24) Until now you have asked for nothing in My name; ask and you will receive, so that your joy may be made full. (25) These things I have spoken to you in figurative language; an hour is coming when I will no longer speak to you in figurative language, but will tell you plainly of the Father. (26) In that day you will ask in My name, and I do not say to you that I will request of the Father on your behalf; (27) for the Father Himself loves you, because you have loved Me and have believed that I came forth from the Father. (28) I came forth from the Father and have come into the world; I am leaving the world again and going to the Father." (29) His disciples said, "Lo, now You are speaking plainly and are not using a figure of speech. (30) Now we know that You know all things, and have no need for anyone to question You; by this we believe that You came from God." (31) Jesus answered them, "Do you now believe? (32) Behold, an hour is coming, and has already come, for you to be scattered, each to his own home, and to leave Me alone; and yet I am not alone, because the Father is with Me. (33) These things I have spoken to you, so that in Me you may have peace. In the world you have tribulation, but take courage; I have overcome the world."

1B Devotion to God (17:1-26)

[*Chapter 17*] (1) Jesus spoke these things; and lifting up His eyes to heaven, He said, "Father, the hour has come; glorify Your Son, that the Son may glorify You, (2) even as You gave Him authority over all flesh, that to all whom You have given Him, He may give eternal life. (3) This is eternal life, that they may know You, the only true God, and Jesus Christ whom You have sent. (4) I glorified You on the earth, having accomplished the work which You have given Me to do. (5) Now, Father, glorify Me together with Yourself, with the glory which I had with You before the world was. (6) I have manifested Your name to the men whom You gave Me out of the world; they were Yours and You gave them to Me, and they have kept Your word. (7) Now they have come to know that everything You have given Me is from You; (8) for the words which You gave Me I have given to them; and they received them and truly understood that I came forth from You, and they believed that You sent Me. (9) I ask on their behalf; I do not ask on behalf of the world, but of those whom You have given Me; for they are Yours; (10) and all things that are Mine are Yours, and Yours are Mine; and I have been glorified in them. (11) I am no longer in the world; and yet they themselves are in the world, and I come to You. Holy Father, keep them in Your name, the name which You have given Me, that they may be one even as We are. (12) While I was with them, I was keeping them in Your name which You have given Me; and I guarded them and not one of them perished but the son of perdition, so that the Scripture would be fulfilled. (13) But now I come to You; and these things I speak in the world so that they may have My joy made full in themselves. (14) I have given them Your word; and the world has hated them, because they are not of the world, even as I am not of the world. (15) I do not ask You to take them out of the world, but to keep them from the evil one. (16) They are not of the world, even as I am not of the world. (17) Sanctify them in the truth; Your word is truth. (18) As You sent Me into the world, I also have sent them into the world. (19) For their sakes I sanctify Myself, that they themselves also may be sanctified in truth. (20) I do not ask on behalf of these alone, but for those also who believe in Me through their word; (21) that they may all be one; even as You, Father, are in Me and I in You, that they also may be in Us, so that the world may believe that You sent Me. (22) The glory which You have given Me I have given to them, that they may be one, just as We are one; (23) I in them and You in Me, that they may be perfected in unity, so that the world may know that You sent Me, and loved them, even as You have loved Me. (24) Father, I desire that they also, whom You have given Me, be with Me where I am, so that they may see My glory which You have given Me, for You loved Me before the foundation of the world. (25) O righteous Father, although the world has not known You, yet I have known You; and these have known that You sent Me; (26) and I have made Your name known to them, and will make it known, so that the love with which You loved Me may be in them, and I in them."

WRITE YOUR OWN EULOGY

Our English word eulogy comes from the Greek word *eulogia* meaning to speak well of, to bless. To help you think about and prepare for what's ahead on the labyrinth of leadership, write a eulogy (especially about your life as a pastor) that you would want read at your memorial service.

Following are some points to consider as you outline or manuscript your own pastoral eulogy:

- Keep the tone positive. (Remember the meaning of *eulogia*!)
- Why were you a pastor? (Recall your call to ministry.)
- What spiritual gifts did God give you?
- Did you have a life verse? A favorite passage or book of the Bible?
- What were major themes in your ministry? ("Pastor would always say, . . .")
- Do you have a treasured memory as a pastor? A word of encouragement you never forgot?
- How did you define success? (Share a success story.)
- Summarize your knowledge of God and self.
- How did you finish well? What prepared you to finish the course and keep the faith?
- What is your legacy? What will people miss most by your absence?

MY EULOGY
(Initial Thoughts)

_____

_____

_____

_____

_____

_____

_____

_____

_____

_____

(See an example on the next page)

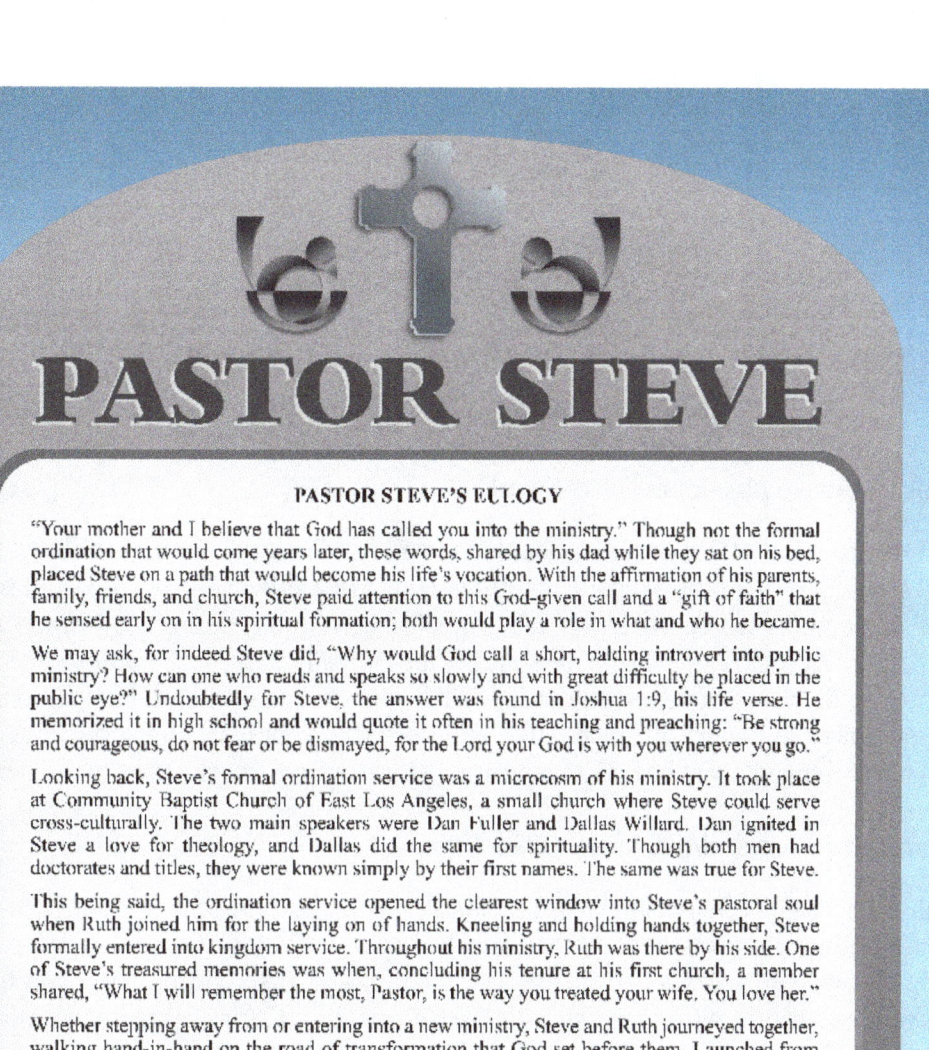

PASTOR STEVE'S EULOGY

"Your mother and I believe that God has called you into the ministry." Though not the formal ordination that would come years later, these words, shared by his dad while they sat on his bed, placed Steve on a path that would become his life's vocation. With the affirmation of his parents, family, friends, and church, Steve paid attention to this God-given call and a "gift of faith" that he sensed early on in his spiritual formation; both would play a role in what and who he became.

We may ask, for indeed Steve did, "Why would God call a short, balding introvert into public ministry? How can one who reads and speaks so slowly and with great difficulty be placed in the public eye?" Undoubtedly for Steve, the answer was found in Joshua 1:9, his life verse. He memorized it in high school and would quote it often in his teaching and preaching: "Be strong and courageous, do not fear or be dismayed, for the Lord your God is with you wherever you go."

Looking back, Steve's formal ordination service was a microcosm of his ministry. It took place at Community Baptist Church of East Los Angeles, a small church where Steve could serve cross-culturally. The two main speakers were Dan Fuller and Dallas Willard. Dan ignited in Steve a love for theology, and Dallas did the same for spirituality. Though both men had doctorates and titles, they were known simply by their first names. The same was true for Steve.

This being said, the ordination service opened the clearest window into Steve's pastoral soul when Ruth joined him for the laying on of hands. Kneeling and holding hands together, Steve formally entered into kingdom service. Throughout his ministry, Ruth was there by his side. One of Steve's treasured memories was when, concluding his tenure at his first church, a member shared, "What I will remember the most, Pastor, is the way you treated your wife. You love her."

Whether stepping away from or entering into a new ministry, Steve and Ruth journeyed together, walking hand-in-hand on the road of transformation that God set before them. Launched from their diverse backgrounds, they founded RobbinsNest Ministries with a unified burden for pastors and missionaries. This proved to be Steve's life mission. With each passing year it became clearer that he was called to advance Christian spiritual formation in pastors and churches.

Steve's passion was to expand people's vision of God, build their intention to be disciples of Jesus, and engage them in spiritual disciplines, or as he would call them, "transforming habits." Through his writing, teaching, and mentoring, Steve clarified the Christian life for those he influenced, often using acrostics to do so! Though frequently clashing with the voices of the modern experts, his commitment to the historic faith and practices was refreshing, if not prophetic.

So how did he remain faithful, especially being so counter-cultural to the market-driven, ever-evolving American church? What held him together? Steve would be the first to acknowledge that it was the grace of God. God gifted him with faith, family, and friends. Whether he was doing domestic or international work, Steve was most alive, effective, and joy-filled when he served side-by-side with his wife, kids, and life-long friends. His success was in his faithfulness.

In this age of uncertainty and triviality, that may be what we will miss and seek to emulate the most. For Steve, a life well lived was one lived authentically from the inside out. He truly experienced the blessings of an ongoing, interactive, ever-deepening relationship with Jesus. With humility, he magnified his pastoral office and sought to be one in whom Christ dwelled and was well pleased. May Steve now reign in peace (R.I.P.) with Him—to God's glory and his joy!

RobbinsNest Ministries
Stop. Look. Listen.

"I MAGNIFY MY OFFICE" (ROMANS 11:13).
Litany of Affirmation

Pastors, what you do is significant.

There is dignity to our calling. Almighty God chose us to be a part of His kingdom work.

As pastors, you are physicians of the soul.

Although the pastoral office has been secularized and defined as running a church, we believe the Puritans' term "physician of the soul" captures what we are because we look out for the spiritual health of those entrusted to our care. We work for their progress and joy in the faith. We help them expand their vision of who God is and what He calls them to be and to do. We build their intention to be disciples of Jesus, students-for-life who learn from Him how to live and love. We help them engage in means of grace—like solitude, study, prayer, and service. As physicians of the soul, we help people see how God is writing His story on the pages of their lives.

As pastors, you are administrators of the keys.

Although "the pastor" increasingly depreciates into a figurehead, we believe we execute true power as administrators of the keys because we open and close God's kingdom doors through preaching the gospel, administering the sacraments, and disciplining the church. We give the blessed welcome to life with God through God-glorifying, Christ-centered, Spirit-led preaching. Also, God has placed us in charge of the sacraments—the rites and services of the holy, universal church. As administrators of the keys, we use the keys to open and close the doors to people's thoughts, attitudes, and actions. With humility, we confront and correct the body of Christ.

As pastors, you are shepherds of the ekklesia.

Although the image of "shepherd" is viewed as pre-modern and even archaic, we believe it remains a valid and useful metaphor to describe us today because a "pastor" by definition leads, feeds, and cares for God's people. We are given the high calling to "shepherd the church of God which He purchased with His own blood." Though we may have titles like "Leader," "Minister," and "Reverend," the title "Pastor" best captures the principal, unifying image of what we are—shepherds of the ekklesia, the called-out ones.

As pastors, you are teachers of the truth.

Although academia relegates the Christian faith to the realm of treasured traditions, personal opinions, or blind commitments, we believe we are teachers of the truth because we dwell in the knowledge of what actually is and bring that reality to others as God's spokespeople. More so than anyone, we are best positioned to be teachers of the nations—to bring a worldview to the global table and answer Pilate's ageless question, "What is truth?" As teachers of the truth, we help people see that what is real is the triune God and His kingdom, that those who are blessed are those who live a with-God life, that a truly good person is one pervaded with servant love, and that one becomes a truly good person by surrendering unto and following Jesus.

As pastors, you are overseers of the church.

Although business measures the boss's success by "the bottom line," we believe that "bodies, buildings, and bucks" are the blessings, not benchmarks, of our office because we are overseers of the church. We are stewards of kingdom resources, watchmen on the wall, guardians of the faith. We watch over and protect the church. We make sure that orthodoxy and orthopraxy is taught to all age groups. We keep the staff accountable and equipped. We champion unity in the body of Christ. We insist that the church be a good steward of her facilities, finances, and calendar of events. And, as overseers of the church, we guard and defend her reputation.

As pastors, you are role models of holiness.

Although a "holier than thou" attitude is to be avoided, we believe we are to take seriously the commands "Come out from their midst and be separate" and "Be perfect, as your heavenly Father is perfect" because we are role models of holiness. People inside and outside the church are watching us. One of their greatest needs is our holiness. Both in our public and private lives, we "prove to be examples to the flock" and to the wolves. As role models of holiness, we welcome accountability, spiritual discipline, and prayer-filled lives.

Pastors, what you do is significant.

Amen—to God be the glory!

OLIVET DISCOURSE
(Matthew 24–25)

LEARNING "SIGN" LANGUAGE

[*Matthew 24*] (1) Jesus came out from the temple and was going away when His disciples came up to point out the temple buildings to Him. (2) And He said to them, "Do you not see all these things? Truly I say to you, not one stone here will be left upon another, which will not be torn down." (3) As He was sitting on the Mount of Olives, the disciples came to Him privately, saying, "Tell us, when will these things happen, and what will be the sign of Your coming, and of the end of the age?" (4) And Jesus answered and said to them, "See to it that no one misleads you. (5) For many will come in My name, saying, 'I am the Christ,' and will mislead many. (6) You will be hearing of wars and rumors of wars. See that you are not frightened, for those things must take place, but that is not yet the end. (7) For nation will rise against nation, and kingdom against kingdom, and in various places there will be famines and earthquakes. (8) But all these things are merely the beginning of birth pangs. (9) Then they will deliver you to tribulation, and will kill you, and you will be hated by all nations because of My name. (10) At that time many will fall away and will betray one another and hate one another. (11) Many false prophets will arise and will mislead many. (12) Because lawlessness is increased, most people's love will grow cold. (13) But the one who endures to the end, he will be saved. (14) This gospel of the kingdom shall be preached in the whole world as a testimony to all the nations, and then the end will come.

PLAN ON & FOR TRIBULATION

(15) Therefore when you see the abomination of desolation which was spoken of through Daniel the prophet, standing in the holy place (let the reader understand), (16) then those who are in Judea must flee to the mountains. (17) Whoever is on the housetop must not go down to get the things out that are in his house. (18) Whoever is in the field must not turn back to get his cloak. (19) But woe to those who are pregnant and to those who are nursing babies in those days! (20) But pray that your flight will not be in the winter, or on a Sabbath. (21) For then there will be a great tribulation, such as has not occurred since the beginning of the world until now, nor ever

will. (22) Unless those days had been cut short, no life would have been saved; but for the sake of the elect those days will be cut short. (23) Then if anyone says to you, 'Behold, here is the Christ,' or 'There He is,' do not believe him. (24) For false Christs and false prophets will arise and will show great signs and wonders, so as to mislead, if possible, even the elect. (25) Behold, I have told you in advance. (26) So if they say to you, 'Behold, He is in the wilderness,' do not go out, or, 'Behold, He is in the inner rooms,' do not believe them. (27) For just as the lightning comes from the east and flashes even to the west, so will the coming of the Son of Man be. (28) Wherever the corpse is, there the vultures will gather.

SAVE THE WAILS us from

(29) But immediately after the tribulation of those days the sun will be darkened, and the moon will not give its light, and the stars will fall from the sky, and the powers of the heavens will be shaken. (30) And then the sign of the Son of Man will appear in the sky, and then all the tribes of the earth will mourn, and they will see the Son of Man coming on the clouds of the sky with power and great glory. (31) And He will send forth His angels with a great trumpet and they will gather together His elect from the four winds, from one end of the sky to the other. (32) Now learn the parable from the fig tree: when its branch has already become tender and puts forth its leaves, you know that summer is near; (33) so, you too, when you see all these things, recognize that He is near, right at the door. (34) Truly I say to you, this generation will not pass away until all these things take place. (35) Heaven and earth will pass away, but My words will not pass away.

THREE PARABLES, ONE MESSAGE

(36) But of that day and hour no one knows, not even the angels of heaven, nor the Son, but the Father alone. (37) For the coming of the Son of Man will be just like the days of Noah. (38) For as in those days before the flood they were eating and drinking, marrying and giving in marriage, until the day that Noah entered the ark, (39) and they did not understand until the flood came and took them all away; so will the coming of the Son of Man be. (40) Then there will be two men in the field; one will be taken and one will be left. (41) Two women will be grinding at the mill; one will be taken and one will be left. (42) Therefore be on the alert, for you do not know which day your Lord is coming. (43) But be sure of this, that if the head of the house had known at

what time of the night the thief was coming, he would have been on the alert and would not have allowed his house to be broken into. (44) For this reason you also must be ready; for the Son of Man is coming at an hour when you do not think He will. (45) Who then is the faithful and sensible slave whom his master put in charge of his household to give them their food at the proper time? (46) Blessed is that slave whom his master finds so doing when he comes. (47) Truly I say to you that he will put him in charge of all his possessions. (48) But if that evil slave says in his heart, 'My master is not coming for a long time,' (49) and begins to beat his fellow slaves and eat and drink with drunkards; (50) the master of that slave will come on a day when he does not expect him and at an hour which he does not know, (51) and will cut him in pieces and assign him a place with the hypocrites; in that place there will be weeping and gnashing of teeth.

EXTRA VIRGIN'S OIL

[*Matthew 25*] (1) Then the kingdom of heaven will be comparable to ten virgins, who took their lamps and went out to meet the bridegroom. (2) Five of them were foolish, and five were prudent. (3) For when the foolish took their lamps, they took no oil with them, (4) but the prudent took oil in flasks along with their lamps. (5) Now while the bridegroom was delaying, they all got drowsy and began to sleep. (6) But at midnight there was a shout, 'Behold, the bridegroom! Come out to meet him.' (7) Then all those virgins rose and trimmed their lamps. (8) The foolish said to the prudent, 'Give us some of your oil, for our lamps are going out.' (9) But the prudent answered, 'No, there will not be enough for us and you too; go instead to the dealers and buy some for yourselves.' (10) And while they were going away to make the purchase, the bridegroom came, and those who were ready went in with him to the wedding feast; and the door was shut. (11) Later the other virgins also came, saying, 'Lord, lord, open up for us.' (12) But he answered, 'Truly I say to you, I do not know you.' (13) Be on the alert then, for you do not know the day nor the hour.

TRANSFORMING TALENTS

(14) For it is just like a man about to go on a journey, who called his own slaves and entrusted his possessions to them. (15) To one he gave five talents, to another, two, and to another, one, each according to his own ability; and he went on his journey. (16) Immediately the one who had

received the five talents went and traded with them, and gained five more talents. (17) In the same manner the one who had received the two talents gained two more. (18) But he who received the one talent went away, and dug a hole in the ground and hid his master's money. (19) Now after a long time the master of those slaves came and settled accounts with them. (20) The one who had received the five talents came up and brought five more talents, saying, 'Master, you entrusted five talents to me. See, I have gained five more talents.' (21) His master said to him, 'Well done, good and faithful slave. You were faithful with a few things, I will put you in charge of many things; enter into the joy of your master.' (22) Also the one who had received the two talents came up and said, 'Master, you entrusted two talents to me. See, I have gained two more talents.' (23) His master said to him, 'Well done, good and faithful slave. You were faithful with a few things, I will put you in charge of many things; enter into the joy of your master.' (24) And the one also who had received the one talent came up and said, 'Master, I knew you to be a hard man, reaping where you did not sow and gathering where you scattered no seed. (25) And I was afraid, and went away and hid your talent in the ground. See, you have what is yours.' (26) But his master answered and said to him, 'You wicked, lazy slave, you knew that I reap where I did not sow and gather where I scattered no seed. (27) Then you ought to have put my money in the bank, and on my arrival I would have received my money back with interest. (28) Therefore take away the talent from him, and give it to the one who has the ten talents.' (29) For to everyone who has, more shall be given, and he will have an abundance; but from the one who does not have, even what he does have shall be taken away. (30) Throw out the worthless slave into the outer darkness; in that place there will be weeping and gnashing of teeth.

SHEEP AND GOATS

(31) But when the Son of Man comes in His glory, and all the angels with Him, then He will sit on His glorious throne. (32) All the nations will be gathered before Him; and He will separate them from one another, as the shepherd separates the sheep from the goats; (33) and He will put the sheep on His right, and the goats on the left. (34) Then the King will say to those on His right, 'Come, you who are blessed of My Father, inherit the kingdom prepared for you from the foundation of the world. 35 For I was hungry, and you gave Me something to eat; I was thirsty, and you gave Me something to drink; I was a stranger, and you invited Me in; (36) naked, and you clothed Me; I was sick, and you visited Me; I was in prison, and you came to Me.' (37) Then

the righteous will answer Him, 'Lord, when did we see You hungry, and feed You, or thirsty, and give You something to drink? (38) And when did we see You a stranger, and invite You in, or naked, and clothe You? (39) When did we see You sick, or in prison, and come to You?' (40) The King will answer and say to them, 'Truly I say to you, to the extent that you did it to one of these brothers of Mine, even the least of them, you did it to Me.' (41) Then He will also say to those on His left, 'Depart from Me, accursed ones, into the eternal fire which has been prepared for the devil and his angels; (42) for I was hungry, and you gave Me nothing to eat; I was thirsty, and you gave Me nothing to drink; (43) I was a stranger, and you did not invite Me in; naked, and you did not clothe Me; sick, and in prison, and you did not visit Me.' (44) Then they themselves also will answer, 'Lord, when did we see You hungry, or thirsty, or a stranger, or naked, or sick, or in prison, and did not take care of You?' (45) Then He will answer them, 'Truly I say to you, to the extent that you did not do it to one of the least of these, you did not do it to Me.' (46) These will go away into eternal punishment, but the righteous into eternal life."

RobbinsNest Ministries
Stop. Look. Listen.

THE FIFTY-TWO
"ALTHOUGH . . . ROBBINSNEST THINKS . . . BECAUSE . . ."
THESIS STATEMENTS

Although "trend-winds" of change sway the targets of success and confuse both clergy and laity, RobbinsNest thinks a pastor's labor focuses to see Christ formed in themselves *and* their people because this is the essence of and pathway to "progress and joy in the faith" (Philippians 1:25).

Although we are not prone to dwell on or even consider the idea of Jesus having a comedic sense, RobbinsNest thinks it is important to recapture the true humanity and winsomeness of our Lord because love for neighbor will not fully happen until all characteristics of Christ be formed in us.

Although the gospel gets reduced to "pray this prayer so that when you die you go to heaven," RobbinsNest thinks being born from above anticipates having holy habits be operational in us because salvation involves giving God our life (not just our death) and seeing Christ formed in us.

Although the burden to succeed and the need to please "seekers" presides over today's pastors, RobbinsNest thinks pastors can abandon outcomes to God and have restful trust realized in them because, like Him whom they're yoked to, they have a Father who works for, in, and through them.

Although self-help gurus encourage us to experiment with new identities when finding ourselves, RobbinsNest thinks an integrated self, one that's whole and authentic, must be maintained in us because being Christ-formed encompasses all of our parts, every dimension of our human lives.

Although the third member of the Trinity is often misunderstood, downplayed, or even ignored, RobbinsNest thinks the Holy Spirit's leading is to be embodied (welcomed and manifested) in us because kingdom living is "righteousness, peace, and joy in the Holy Spirit" (Romans 14:17).

Although religious systems often prioritize dogmas and rules of order that keep outsiders outside, RobbinsNest thinks that table fellowship, as seen in Jesus *the* pastor, will be deliberate in us because the law of love repositions us to pay attention to and break bread with our "neighbor."

Although conferences help you DO things like "develop your brand" and "determine your price," RobbinsNest thinks that faithful pastors are first and foremost called to BE things like "in Christ" because only from this reality can one journey through this life and the next and bear good fruit.

Although a plethora of advice (books, webinars, conferences, etc.) bombards emerging leaders, RobbinsNest thinks Jesus' Upper Room Discourse offers the greatest leadership advice bar none because in it He—the greatest leader ever to live—constructs the framework for building leaders.

Although titles, degrees, and honors have their place in the pastorate, RobbinsNest thinks humble service to others makes a kingdom leader because *the* Pastor-Leader "did not come to be served, but to serve" (Matt. 20:28) and "emptied Himself, taking the form of a bond-servant" (Phil. 2:7).

Although many in leadership justify meanness and act as if it is better to be right than to be good, RobbinsNest thinks kingdom leaders will confront with care and progressively become like Jesus (who was/is right and good) because they are role models of holiness and loyal to truth and love.

Although private enterprise and "pull-yourself-up-by-the-bootstraps" philosophy has its place in this world, RobbinsNest thinks that true kingdom leaders abide in Christ and submit to His word and will because, in the kingdom of God, they work in a power that is not their own or natural.

Although innovative and efficient techniques and irrefutable laws may build corporate leaders, RobbinsNest thinks the central material needed for building kingdom leaders is a *fruit-bearing friend of Jesus* because apart from Him we can do nothing that bears good and lasting fruit.

Although this dog-eat-dog world awards ambitious people who make a name for themselves, RobbinsNest thinks kingdom leaders are built by a contrasting and forward thinking worldview because they, like their Lord, sojourn as outcasts in this world with eternity in their hearts.

Although modernity purports that God is either dead or too busy or detached to care or relate to us, RobbinsNest thinks we are wise to listen with care for God to speak and communicate with us because He is not only alive, but He has given us life so that we may have fellowship with Him.

Although pushy marketeers and personalities may turn around plateau or declining churches, RobbinsNest thinks that Jesuslike prayer and devotion to God builds God-glorifying churches because the kingdom of God, in which *the* Church resides, is born from above, not manmade.

Although today's "image-is-everything" baits us to create brands and live mile-wide, inch-deep lives, RobbinsNest thinks pastors and churches are to be faithful to their calling with core values intact and intentional because the Christian life is deep and weighty and for the glory of God.

Although a cultural shift toward "tolerance" and "change" evolves, RobbinsNest thinks Christ-Centeredness is a core value to uphold because "Jesus Christ is Lord" was the church's earliest confession (Philippians 2:11), continues to be true today, and will forever be what actually is so.

Although a flippant fascination with "new and improved" stirs the economy, RobbinsNest thinks orthodoxy and orthopraxy—two sides of the same *koinonia*—form a core value to treasure because established right belief and practice unite the communion of saints, both past and present.

Although pastors and church members are often appraised and praised by how much time they spend at the church, RobbinsNest thinks optimal ministry is mobile because God's kingdom mission for us (the *missio regni Dei*) is to "Go" forth and invite people into a life with God.

Although cynicism is the present product produced by the plethora of programs promising the "key" for success, RobbinsNest thinks there is indeed a reliable path for spiritual formation because "Vision-Intention-Means" has proved to be fruitful, not faddish, for real transformation.

Although consultants advise "Go for the market" and tout profit margins, RobbinsNest thinks kingdom goods and services should be, among other things, affordable and accessible because, as Jesus said, "It is more blessed to give than to receive" and "Freely you received, freely give."

Although church consultants often treat small churches as a problem that God wants to fix, RobbinsNest thinks they are a strategy God uses to bring about His kingdom purpose because they are consistent with how He has operated His divine conspiracy throughout holy history.

Although "God is dead" or at least irrelevant is peddled in the public square, RobbinsNest thinks "*Soli Deo Gloria*" is a core value to commend because this is a God-bathed, God-permeated world where He is the prime mover and sustainer, the most alive and relevant inhabitant and hero.

Although jokes about pastors are in vogue and many in and out of the church belittle their position, RobbinsNest thinks it is high time to magnify the office of pastor and to dignify their sacred call because they are shepherds of the very ones that God purchased with His own blood (Acts 20:28)!

Although the pastoral office has been secularized and homogenized, debased and defined as running a church, RobbinsNest thinks the Puritans' term "physician of the soul" captures what a pastor is because a pastor looks out for the spiritual health of those entrusted to his care.

Although "the pastor" increasingly depreciates into a figurehead, RobbinsNest thinks the pastor executes true power as an "administrator of the keys" because he opens and closes God's kingdom doors through preaching the gospel, administering the sacraments, and disciplining the church.

Although the image of "shepherd" is viewed as pre-modern and even archaic, RobbinsNest thinks it remains a valid and useful metaphor to describe the contemporary pastor because a "pastor" (*poimen*) by definition leads, feeds, and cares for the ekklesia (i.e., God's called-out ones).

Although academia relegates the Christian "faith" to the realm of treasured traditions, personal opinions, or blind commitments, RobbinsNest thinks pastors are "teachers of the truth" because they dwell in the knowledge of what actually is and bring that reality to others as God's spokesmen.

Although business measures the boss's success by "the bottom line," RobbinsNest thinks that "bodies, buildings, and bucks" (i.e., the ABCs of church growth: *a*ttendance, *b*uildings, and *c*ash) are the blessings, not benchmarks, of the pastor's office because he is an overseer of the church.

Although a "holier than thou" attitude is to be avoided, RobbinsNest thinks pastors are to take seriously the commands "Come out from their midst and be separate" (2 Corinthians 6:17) and "Be perfect, as your heavenly Father is perfect" (Matthew 5:48) because they are role models of holiness.

Although "end times" is big business that feeds on narcissistic curiosity and misleads the masses, RobbinsNest thinks we are to practice what Jesus preached on end times (e.g., Olivet Discourse) because biblical eschatology serves, shapes, and schools our here and now spiritual formation.

Although the mindset of "we'll cross that bridge when it comes" and avoiding conflict is tempting, RobbinsNest thinks that *preparation* for the long obedience is one of Jesus' "Eschamation Points" because trials and tribulations are foreordained and inescapable until the final "Day of the Lord."

Although a growing number of Christian leaders act as if it is better to be right than to be good, RobbinsNest thinks that self-examination-driven *repentance* is one of Jesus' Eschamation Points because—in the end—"Well done, good and faithful servant" is not a grade on a doctrine exam.

Although the world around us increasingly inclines the majority to grow cynical and materialistic, RobbinsNest thinks *encouragement* (both received and given) is one of Jesus' Eschamation Points because life in God's kingdom is open to us now (and not just for the übermystical among us).

Although "end times" can feed curiosity (which is said to be the first step on the ladder of pride), RobbinsNest thinks *adoration*—not some figure-it-out-ism—is one of Jesus' Eschamation Points because a hymn book, not a crystal ball, takes us up and into God's grand story and our chief end.

Although "Everyone did what was right in his own eyes" (Judges 21:25) is applauded today, RobbinsNest thinks *community*—a life with and for others—is one of Jesus' Eschamation Points because, from the beginning in the garden to the end-times and beyond, life is not a private event.

Although being "in-the-know" and even forcing the hand of God can label a leader "ambitious," RobbinsNest thinks *humility* that abandons outcomes to God is one of Jesus' Eschamation Points because God—the One who is guiding history—is writing His story on the pages of our lives.

Although the present state of the church leaves many leaders hopeless, RobbinsNest thinks these are extraordinary times to be kingdom pastors because, to echo Dallas Willard's prophetic voice, "We are on the verge of a time when the church is going to be able to make some decisions."

Although jokes about ministers are in vogue and many outside and inside the church belittle the position of pastor, RobbinsNest Ministries thinks it's time to magnify the office of pastor because they are called—as sent ambassadors—to "shepherd the flock of God among you" (1 Peter 5:2)!

Although pastors are hired with and evaluated by the expectation to take the church "to the next level," RobbinsNest thinks that business-driven results are unrealistic and counterproductive because God's kingdom pastors only work effectively in the power that is not their own or natural.

Although many see outreach and worship as a marketing strategy, RobbinsNest thinks that pastors should evangelize the church and work with the people who are there because discipleship is the primary mission of the church (and is, in fact, what truly fuels worship and outreach).

Although common belief asserts that you can be a Christian without being a disciple, RobbinsNest thinks discipleship constitutes the Christian life because Jesus' call is to trust Him with your life, not just your death, and to learn from Him how to love God and neighbor in everyday life.

Although doubt is considered virtuous and truth is seen as evolving in this post-modern world, RobbinsNest thinks that pastors are best positioned to preach and teach true and abiding knowledge about the availability and desirability of God's kingdom because that's what Jesus did.

Although culture advocates mass-production and quick fixes, RobbinsNest thinks pastors should invest the time to expand peoples' vision of God, build their intention to be Jesus' disciples, and promote the means of grace because this forms the reliable pattern for spiritual formation.

Although most organizations focus on and stress over the outcomes and results of their events, RobbinsNest thinks there is a better and more HONEST way to approach events when evaluating because God calls us to be faithful and to entrust the results and abandon the outcomes to Him.

Although statistics show that 50% of those who go into fulltime ministry will no longer be in ministry five years later, RobbinsNest thinks pastors can flourish and finish well because God routinely showers His amazing grace upon those who develop an enduring focus to their calling.

Although pop-Christianity sees spirituality as a wave to ride now or an option to consider later, RobbinsNest thinks the coming of spirituality in Jesus—*adventuality*—is at hand and to be hailed because being with Jesus to become like Jesus is "*the* Way," not a passing wave, of Christianity.

Although the bifurcation of justification and sanctification minimizes the latter in some theological camps, RobbinsNest thinks spiritual formation is central to salvation because your "progress and joy in the faith" (Philippians 1:25) continues "until Christ is formed in you" (Galatians 4:19).

Although crowds of time-wasters and hedon-chasers contend with their wayward, unruly lives, RobbinsNest thinks pastors and churches work best with a "rule" for life in place and in process because God designed us to live out our numbered days here on earth with wisdom and strength.

Although publishers saturate the market with the latest experts' must-have leadership ideologies, RobbinsNest thinks budding and veteran leaders need only to look to Jesus' teaching and example because He has the best information on the most important topics, including what's a leader to do.

Although the expected and celebrated pace of modern ministry remains conducive to a racetrack, RobbinsNest thinks pastors must slow down and relentlessly eliminate hurry from their lives because the pace of grace creates space and time for God to act in the labyrinth of leadership.

WORKS CITED

Baxter, Richard. *The Reformed Pastor*. Carlisle, PA: Banner of Truth Trust, 1997.

Bruner, Frederick Dale. *Matthew, a Commentary*. Vol. 2. Dallas: Word, 1990.

Dawn, Marva and Eugene Peterson. *The Unnecessary Pastor*. Grand Rapids, MI: Wm. B. Eerdmans, 2000.

Herbert, George. *The Country Parson, The Temple*. Mahwah, NJ: Paulist, 1981.

Lewis, C. S. *Mere Christianity*. New York: Macmillan, 1958.

_____. *The Screwtape Letters*. New York: Macmillan, 1961.

Peterson, Eugene H. *The Contemplative Pastor*. Dallas: Word, 1989.

Reuben, Julie A. *The Making of the Modern University*. Chicago: University of Chicago Press, 1996.

Robbins, Stephen W. *Transforming Beliefs: Spiritual Guidance through the Apostles' Creed*. Eugene, OR: Wipf and Stock, 2006.

Sanders, J. Oswald. *Spiritual Leadership*. Chicago: Moody, 1994.

Spurgeon, Charles Haddon. *Lectures to My Students*. Grand Rapids, MI: Zondervan, 1996.

Thomas à Kempis. *The Imitation of Christ*. Translated by Leo Sherley-Price. New York: Penguin Books, 1952.

Wesley, Charles. "And Can It Be?" in *Praise! Our Songs and Hymns*. Grand Rapids, MI: Zondervan, 1983.

Willard, Dallas. *Knowing Christ Today*. New York: HarperCollins, 2009.

_____. *Living in Christ Presence*. Downers Grove, IL: InterVarsity, 2014.

_____. *The Divine Conspiracy*. San Francisco: HarperSanFrancisco, 1998.

> RobbinsNest Ministries has the grace of being overseen by someone who has spent years looking into the matters of spiritual disciplines and how they relate to spiritual growth. It really is not just enough to stagger along, trying to find something that will help here and something that will help there. The history of the church is full of rich wisdom about all these matters. Steve Robbins is a person who has actually studied this at great length and has written on it and has put it into practice in his own life. And, therefore, his supervision of not only the operation but the individuals who come into RobbinsNest Ministries is, I believe, going to be significant for the future of ministry in this area.
> —Dallas Willard

Drs. Steve and Ruth Robbins founded RobbinsNest Ministries at the turn of the new millennium.

Mission

This fully recognized 501(c)(3) organization exists to . . .

- "Advance Christian spiritual formation in pastors and churches around the world."

Goal

The goal is to . . .

- Focus and expand their *vision* of God
- Build up their *intention* to live as disciples of Jesus
- Promote the *means* of classic spiritual disciplines

Method

Throughout the year the ministry . . .

- Mentors pastors one-to-one
- Facilitates clergy small groups
- Trains seminarians and interns
- Runs an institute for "spirituality and ministry"
- Leads retreats
- Provides resources

Please visit www.RobbinsNestMinistries.org to discover more about RobbinsNest Ministries.

BOOKS BY STEPHEN W. ROBBINS

Theology by itself is not wisdom. Doctrine is not automatically knowledge. What constitutes wisdom and knowledge is an interactive relationship with God, a life that abides in His presence and takes on His character. Stephen W. Robbins states in the Preface, "My intention for writing this book is not to merely transfer information from my brain to yours. How sad would that be! I want to help you be a transformed (not just an informed) believer."

Transforming Beliefs presents an accessible and straightforward study of the Apostles' Creed. Each chapter addresses one of the affirmations in this statement of faith and concludes with a set of questions and exercises. Designed to help you advance in Christian spiritual formation, this study (1) focuses and expands your vision of who God is and what life looks like in His immediately available kingdom, (2) builds your intention to love God and neighbor in everyday life, and (3) provides you with useful means to do this on your spiritual pilgrimage.

Whether you read it on your own or in a small group, this study of the Apostles' Creed provides spiritual guidance for your journey on the road of transformation.

(Wipf & Stock, 2006)

Human activity, both good and bad, cannot be explained merely by DNA and brain chemistry. Though disappearing in our modern world, moral knowledge is accessible. In His Sermon on the Mount, Jesus teaches how to be a truly good person. With moral authority He describes the good life and gives direction to our will.

Transforming Habits presents an accessible and straightforward study of the Sermon on the Mount. Each chapter addresses one of Jesus' preaching points and ends with a "Sermon Application"—questions to ponder and "transforming habits" (i.e., spiritual disciplines) to practice. Designed to help you live as God intends, this study (1) focuses and expands your vision of what life looks like in His immediately available kingdom, (2) builds your intention to live with Him as a disciple of Jesus, and (3) provides you with useful means to do this in everyday life.

Whether you read it on your own or in a small group, this study of the Sermon on the Mount provides spiritual guidance for your journey on the road of transformation—to God's glory and your joy!

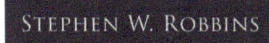

(Wipf & Stock, 2009)

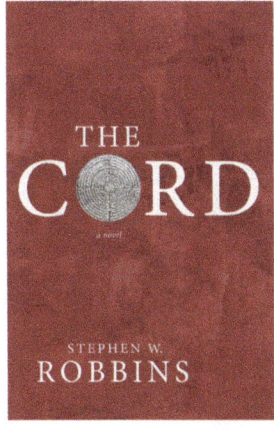

Pastor Payne Donovan was weary to the bone. He often wondered if he made any difference in people's lives or if his church had any impact on the world around him. In the midst of Payne's despair, George Carlson, head of a genetic laboratory called SarkiSystems, offers hope to revive and embolden Payne's ministry by a merging of faith and technology. Dazzled by George's charisma, Payne agrees to go to a meeting and soon finds himself deeply entangled in a plan to revive the faith of the world. But the more Payne invests in the plan, the more broken his family becomes. Pastor Donovan must let go of the hope that SarkiSystems offers in order to find healing for his family and true hope for the world.

(Resource Publications, 2015)

www.ingramcontent.com/pod-product-compliance
Lightning Source LLC
Chambersburg PA
CBHW080547170426
43195CB00016B/2706